PEACOCK BOOKS

Editor: Kaye Webb

PK9

THE COUNTRY CHILD

This is a book about a girl growing up in the country. Alison Uttley has drawn on her own youth to produce memories so vivid and nostalgic that you can almost smell the honeysuckle and hear the owls calling at dusk.

She writes about the small intense joys and sorrows of life on a small farm: the fun of haymaking, the sadness of favourite animals being slaughtered, and the close sweetness of Christmas celebrations in the farmhouse kitchen.

It will delight everyone who enjoys tales of the countryside and its quiet serenity will stay with you long after more conventional stories are forgotten.

For girls (and boys with a taste for poetry) of thirteen and over.

Cover design by Juliet Rennie

ALISON UTTLEY

The Country Child

with illustrations by C. N. Tunnicliffe

PENGUIN BOOKS

Penguin Books Ltd, Harmondsworth, Middlesex
U.S.A.: Penguin Books Inc., 3300 Clipper Mill Road, Baltimore 11, Md
AUSTRALIA: Penguin Books Pty Ltd, 762 Whitehorse Road,
Mitcham, Victoria

—

First published by Faber & Faber 1931
Published in Peacock Books 1963

—

Made and printed in Great Britain
by Richard Clay & Company, Ltd,
Bungay, Suffolk

Set in Monotype Baskerville

The Author's thanks are due to the Editor
of the *Spectator* for permission to reprint an
episode, 'Haymakers', in this book, and also
to the Oxford University Press for the use
of the 'Wassail Song', from *The Oxford Book
of Carols*.

Contents

CHAPTER I

Dark Wood

THE dark wood was green and gold, green where the oak trees stood crowded together with misshapen twisted trunks, red-gold where the great smooth beeches lifted their branching arms to the sky. In between jostled silver birches – olive-tinted fountains which never reached the light – black spruces with little pale candles on each tip, and nut trees smothered to the neck in dense bracken.

The bracken was a forest in itself, a curving verdant flood of branches, transparent as water by the path, but thick, heavy, secret, a foot or two away, where high ferny crests waved above the softly moving ferns, just as the beech tops flaunted above the rest of the wood. The rabbits which crept quietly in and out reared on their hind legs to see who was going by. They pricked their ears and stood erect, and then dropped silently on soft paws and disappeared into the close ranks of brown stems when they saw the child.

She walked along the rough path, casting fearful glances to right and left. She never ran, even in moments of greatest terror, when things seemed very near, for then They would know she was afraid and close round her. Gossamer stretched across the way from nut bush to bracken frond, and clung to her cold cheeks. Split acorns and beech mast lay thick on the ground, green and brown patterns in the upside-down red leaves which made a carpet. Heavy rains had swept the soil to the lower levels of the path, and laid bare the rock in many places. On a sandy patch she saw her own footprint, a little square toe and a horseshoe where the iron heel had sunk. That was in the morning when all was fresh and fair. It cheered her to see the homely mark, and she stayed a moment to look at it, and replace her foot in it, as Robinson Crusoe might have done. A squirrel, rippling along a leafy bough, peered at her, and then, finding her so still, ran down the tree trunk and along the ground.

Her step was strangely silent, and a close observer would have seen that she walked only on the soil between the stones of the footpath, stones of the earth itself, which had worn their way through the thin layer of grass. Her eyes and ears were as alert as those of a small wild animal as she slid through the shades in the depths of the wood. A mis-step made her iron heel catch a stone, and the sharp ring alarmed a blackbird dipping among the beech leaves, but it fright-ened the child still more. She gasped and held her breath, listening with all her senses, her heart beating in her throat. A little breeze rustled, lost among the trees, seeking its parent wind, fluttering the leaves as it tried to escape. Then it flew out through the tree tops and was gone, and she was alone again.

Every day she had this ordeal, a walk of a mile or more through the dense old wood, along the deserted footpath. A hundred years ago, before the highway was made, it was a well-worn road between the villages of Raddle and distant Mellow. Now it only went to Windystone Hall, and every-one walked or drove along the turnpike by the river, deep in the valley, two hundred feet below.

No one ever knew Susan's fears, she never even for-mulated them to herself, except as 'things'. But whether they were giants which she half expected to see straddle out of the dark distance, or dwarfs, hidden behind the trees, or bears and Indians in the undergrowth, or even the trees themselves marching down upon her, she was not certain. They must never be mentioned, and, above all, They must never know she was afraid.

It was no use for her to tell herself there were no giants, or that bears had disappeared in England centuries ago, or that trees could not walk. She knew that quite well, but the terror remained, a subconscious fear which quickly rose to consciousness when she pressed back the catch of the gate at the entrance to the wood, and closed it soundlessly, as she entered the deep listening wood on her way home from school in the dusky evenings.

In the middle of Dark Wood the climbing path rose up a steep incline, too steep for Susan to hurry, with black shadows on either side. Then it skirted a field, a small, queer, haunted-looking field of ragwort and bracken, long given to the wild wood, which pressed in on every side. A high rudely-made wall surrounded it, through the chinks of which she was sure that eyes were watching. To pass this field was the culmination of agony, for she had to walk close to the wall in the semi-darkness of overhanging trees, and nothing could save her if a long arm and skinny hand shot out.

At the top of the field, which sloped up the wood, was a tumbledown building, which was the authentic House that Jack built, with rats and malt complete, but long ago it had been deserted and now Fear lived there. Once she saw a battered man creeping through the bracken towards the ruin, but he never saw the little shadow with a school bag on her back slip past the mossy gate of the field.

Beyond the ragwort field was a fair open stretch of wood, with cow-wheat and delicate fumitory growing by the path. The trees were not so close together, and a glimpse of the blue sky came through in summer, or a star in the winter.

The child's heart ceased its heavy pounding and she took in deep breaths in readiness for the next ordeal, an immense rugged oak tree which waited at the cross-road, where her path cut across two others. One way led downhill to a cottage in the fields below the wood, a path no one used. The other went up the steep sides of the wood past great boulders which lay among the trees like primitive beasts crouching in the dark, until it faded away to nothing in the bracken.

But something was behind the oak tree, hidden, lurking, and the leaves all watched her approach. She threw back

her head and stared boldly at it, but her feet were winged
for flight as she slipped softly along. Once, two years ago,
when she was seven, a pair of eyes had looked at her from
behind the tree, and once a dead white cow had lain there,
swollen and stiff, brought to be buried in the wood.

A nut tree stood in her path, low, human, but it was
friendly, and always she touched its branches with fluttering
trembling fingers, receiving solace from the warm twigs, as
she passed on to meet the oak. She held her head sideways,
pretending to look up at the scrap of sky, but her eyes were
peeping behind, like a scared rabbit's, and the tree seemed
to turn its branches and look after her, whilst the thing,
whatever it was, skipped round the trunk to the other side.
She never turned to look behind her, but trusted to her sense
of hearing, which had become very acute with the strain
imposed upon it. She whispered a little prayer, a cry to God
for help, as she left the tree behind.

Then she walked down the tunnel of beech trees, for the
oaks were left behind and the character of the wood had
changed. The trees thinned and the beeches rose clear of
undergrowth with massive smooth grey trunks from the carpet of golden leaves. Susan breathed naturally again, and
walked rapidly forward, heeding neither rock nor tree, her
eager eyes fixed on the light ahead. The evening sunshine
streamed through the end of the path, a circle of radiance,
where a stile and broken gate ended the wood.

Nothing could get through these, and she sang in a tiny
quavering voice, for she still trembled a little, just to show
the things she didn't care, as she entered the fields beyond.
From the gate it was not far to her home on the hill-top, and
sometimes she could see her mother, standing on a bank,
silhouetted against the sky, anxiously looking for the little
speck of a girl, and waving a teacloth up and down like a
white flag when she saw her come out of the dark doorway of
the wood.

Little Susan Garland walked four miles every morning to
the village school at Dangle. It was the only school, and to it

went the minister's children, the struggling doctor's, the girls
from the saw-mill, boys from the water-mill, children from
remote farms and little manor houses, where they couldn't
afford a governess, children from tiny cottages and small
shops, and rough little people from a long row of stone
dwellings, whose parents lived how they could.

She ran gaily through the Dark Wood without a glance at
the oak tree, or the ragwort field, or the dark patches of
mystery, black even in the morning sunlight. Everything was
asleep and nothing could harm her. The path was downhill,
and she felt free and careless as a squirrel or one of the brown
birds flitting across the fields, very different from the wary,
watchful child who tried to slip unseen through the wood at
night.

Fairy tales always brought her companions, and she
walked homewards down the long road from Dangle to
Raddle with four or five girls hanging round her in a bunch,
arms encircling waists, heads close together, as she told
them of the Princess and the Golden Bird, or the Palace of
Ice. The girls lived at Raddle, a hamlet of pretty thatched
cottages, a post office and a general shop, a mile and a half
from the school and half a mile from the Dark Wood, so
when they were at home Susan had two miles further to go
alone.

When she saw the village approaching and the time for
parting, and the lonely walk through the wood getting near,
she brought her story to a climax and kept it there with the
bribe:

'Walk part way through the wood with me, and I'll tell
you the rest.'

On hot summer afternoons the children came with her
over the bridge, past Lane End Farm, and up the steep fields
which led to the wood. Young stirks and companies of hens
scattered before their laughter and shouts as Susan told her
story. She lured them on into the wood, but soon the silence
and gloom depressed them and they hesitated. 'We must go
home now, it is tea-time, I promised I wouldn't be late,'

they excused themselves uneasily, and back they ran as fast as their legs would go. In the autumn and winter they never put a foot in the wood, and travellers walked round by the road which was a mile longer when they went to Mellow.

As Susan climbed the last hill, on top of which her home was perched so that it looked like a watch-tower against the sky, her mind became calm and her thoughts leapt forward to the house. She walked by the high wall of the orchard, which was covered with berried ivy and clustered with blackberry bushes, but no evil eye stared through its chinks, no face leered from the apple trees. She stopped for breath and looked over the valley laid out like a tapestry of green fields and black walls, dark firs with flat boughs still against the sky, the Dark Wood with its rounded tree-tops curving on the hill-side out of sight, and the little green path disappearing into its solitude. She opened the big white gate, and shut it with a clang behind her, as a challenge, sending the sound down, down, across the fields to the wood to tell 'Them' she was safe.

The yard dog, Roger, barked violently and then changed his frantic rush to a welcoming wag of his whole body as he saw the queer little familiar person skip round the corner, waving her hat and snapping her fingers at him. He stood wistfully looking after her as she walked up the garden through the little wicket gate to the side door. Then he returned to his kennel and lay there, fastened with a heavy chain to the rock at the door of his square stone house, listening, hoping, waiting.

Susan flung open the door of the farmhouse and threw down her bag on the oak dresser.

'Well, have you been a good girl today, Susan?' asked Mrs Garland, as she kissed the warm lips Susan held up to her.

'Yes, Mother, quite good,' said Susan, hesitating.

'Have you had the cane?' continued her mother.

'Yes, for talking, but it didn't hurt,' replied Susan calmly, and she hung her hat and coat behind the door, and washed her hands in the brass bowl standing on the sink.

Mrs Garland set a plate of hot meat and vegetables for her by the bright fire, and as she ate it she told the story of the day's adventures, omitting any reference to her fears in the wood. Even when the girls at school said, 'Aren't you afraid to go through that wood alone, Susan Garland?' she denied it, for it would never do to say her fears aloud, or somehow They would know.

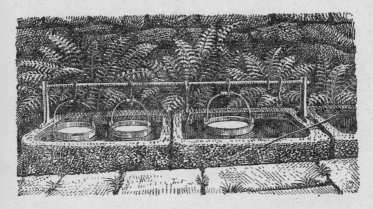

After her meal she played outside in the dusk, running races with herself, skipping up and down the cobbled farm-yard, tossing a ball in the air to hit the sycamore tree, sing-ing and talking to Roger, who ran up and down, nearly wild to get loose. Then she met the farm men walking slowly home with the cans of milk, steadying them with both hands as they swayed on the yokes across their shoulders. She col-lected the eggs from the window ledge in the barn where Becky had left them and carried them to the dairy in a large flat basket. The men put the milk-cans in the stone troughs at the back door to cool whilst they harnessed the horse.

'Susan, Susan, come and stir the milk,' called Tom Gar-land, and Susan ran out and seized a hazel wand which lay, clean and bright, across the troughs. She dipped it in the frothy foamy pails and swirled the milk round and round, sending little splashes of cream over into the water, watching them fall like funnels of opal deep down till they became one with the water. The stars came out and twinkled in the great clean-water trough, and she dipped her wand in to break them into fragments.

'Come on, that's enough. You're spilling the milk and messing the drinking water. Get away, you're no use,' and her father pushed her aside to take the milk to be measured.

Dan took the lantern with him to light his way back from the station, and the cart rattled away down the hill. Tom Garland and Joshua went into the kitchen and Susan ran in too. Margaret lit the lamp and set it in the middle of the table, and they drew up their chairs for tea, but Susan curled up like a kitten in the corner of the settle under the row of shining measures and graters, sieves and colanders. She put her fingers in her ears and lost herself in *Swiss Family Robinson*.

Her library consisted of four books, *Robinson Crusoe*, *Swiss Family Robinson*, *Nicholas Nickleby*, and *Hans Andersen*. She read them in turns, over and over again. This was the sixth time of reading, but the stories were ever new.

The tea things were cleared away, the milk cart returned and Dan sat down to his meal at the end of the dresser by the hall door. Becky washed up the milk-cans and sieves, rattling them on the stone sink, laughing and talking, but Susan read on through all the clatter, even when black shadows fell across her book as people passed between her and the lamp.

At eight o'clock Mrs Garland gave her a little pink mug full of creamy milk and a slice of bread and dripping. She fetched a candle from the old candle-bark in the pantry, and went upstairs to her bed in the attic.

As she left the bright hot kitchen and walked up the stairs she thought of the fox on the landing, the stuffed fox, shot when Susan was a baby by Tom Garland, who found it coming from a hen house. It stood between two windows and its glass eyes followed Susan wherever she went. Never did she lose the feeling that the fox's soul was hidden in his furry body. She could stroke him and touch his eyes with her fingers, and carry him in her arms, but she dare not turn her back on him. So she walked sideways past him, up the stairs to her own bedroom under the roof. The attic stair creaked and she loved the comforting sound, which talked to her. She knew it would cry out if the fox came up in the night.

So she shut the door of the whitewashed room and quickly undressed, whilst her long shadow dipped and mowed and cowered on the crooked ceiling.

It ran over the big mahogany chest of drawers, full of clothes belonging to past generations of Garlands, and hesitated, lingering on the little crib under the eaves where Susan used to sleep with it. It leapt off the carved oak chest, when she put the candlestick to rest there, whilst she washed in the tiny blue and white flowery bowl sunk in the green washstand behind the door. In that oak chest the bride of 'The Mistletoe Bough' had hidden – Old Joshua recited it every Christmas – and her skeleton was found twenty years afterwards by her sorrowing husband. Nothing could shake Susan's belief this was the veritable chest, and she kept a Bible on the top, just in case the bride might lift the lid and pop out.

The window was a tall narrow slit with iron bars, for the attic hung over a cliff with a sheer drop at the back. A great elm tree, growing in the shallow soil which covered the rock, lifted up its boughs and threw in handfuls of yellowing leaves when the window was open. Its murmur always filled the room with whispers, for even on the hottest day its branches waved to and fro, catching every breath of air on that high slope to which it clung, and the little twigs trembled and tapped at the glass.

Down at the bottom of the rock, under the encircling beech wood, rabbits played and stoats crept stealthily from the walls. Often Susan lay with misery in her heart, listening to the piercing screams of the small wild things caught by their enemies, and she sprang out of bed to scare them away. Hawks hovered level with the window, so that she could see their fierce bright eyes before they dropped on a tiny mouse far below. She would creep upstairs when she ought to be peeling potatoes or practising her music, to stare out across the fields and little woods to the tall beech trees which waved their plumy crests against the sky.

But at night, when she had said her prayers and crept into the immense wooden bed with its four round balls like heads at the corners, she could see nothing but the boughs of trees and stars shining through. She lay thinking of the *Swiss Family Robinson*, imagining further adventures in which she was the resourceful heroine, forgetful of the terrors of the day, heedless of the morrow, and so she slept.

CHAPTER 2

Windystone Hall

THE curving, sweeping hillsides dropped down into the narrow little valley where the noisy river, the rapid brown brook, and the white turnpike, with its jingling carts and dusty trudging wayfarers made a pretence of bustle and talk. Then up they climbed, through quiet hollows and dimpled coombes, past little woods and ridged plough-land and soft singing streams, to the heights where the great rocks lay bare and the wind lashed the torn beeches and ragged thorns.

Little flowery fields of every shape and size, square fields, triangles, fish-shaped fields with odd corners, rhomboids, bounded by green hedgerows and black walls, linked arms and ran up hill and down dale, round the folded hills out of sight into countless valleys beyond where the sun set. Woods sprang up everywhere, little fairy woods of silver birches in the dells, bouquets of beech trees, neat and compact on the small round hills, witch woods with streaming hair on the hill-tops, and hundreds of acres of great oak and beech woods which followed the curves of the land and spread up to the sky.

Everywhere green ribbons of lanes and paths threaded the fields and woods, joining valley to valley, tying farm to farm, creeping over the high hills and loitering by the river. Many of these lanes that ran along the crests of the land were the old pack roads; some of them had been traversed by the Romans when they worked the mines which honey-combed the more distant hills, and some were older still, as the savage monoliths and green tumuli in the upland fields attested.

As one looked across the valley, the far villages, hidden among trees in the hollows, could only be distinguished by the faint blue smoke which hung above them, a soft mist against the rolling green. Mellow lay like this, lost in the creases of the hills, until one turned a sudden corner, and found the little stone houses clustering round the duck pond, climbing up the steep rocks and sleeping huddled together about the old market square.

Dangle, too, was sheltered in a hollow where the line of hills doubled back upon itself, miles away, in the woods, with cottages and flower gardens hiding by the stream, and farms nestling under sycamore groves. In between the two villages were a few scattered cottages and farmsteads – the hamlet of Raddle with the small post office and water-mill, the long ridges of dense woods which belonged to the squire, Sir Harry Vane, and the spur on which Susan Garland lived.

The farm, with its stack-yards, buildings, garden, orchard, pig-cotes, and the rambling house itself, looked like an island of fruitfulness, a small Paradise, on a shelf all to itself, with the ground falling or rising on every side. A beech wood swept round the base of the spur, protecting the house from the worst winds, with its great warm trees, and from above the wood the house rose like a fortress.

It was an old farm, Windystone Hall, with buildings dating from Elizabethan times, and foundations older still, but it had been rebuilt, in part, and altered. In a field by the house stood a great black stone, perhaps a monument of ancient times, which, so the story went, walked down to the river to drink whenever it heard the cock crow at midnight. Joshua pointed out that a rock cannot hear, but Susan was not so sure, everything seemed to listen at Windystone.

The gentle cows and great shaggy mares rubbed their sides against it, the sheep lay under its shadow and left wisps of wool which the chaffinches pilfered, and the cock crowed from its level summit as if it were his own barn door.

The long gabled grey stone house was built of the rock

upon which it stood, and became one with the steep crag at
the back, as if it were a tower to resist invaders. Indeed, it
was thought there had once been a Saxon camp there, the
situation was a natural stronghold.

All round were casement windows, diamond-paned and
mullioned, peeping with little twinkling eyes at the smooth
grass plot, the cobbled yard, the garden, the orchard, the
paved paths, and peering down the precipitous rocky slope at
the back over the tops of the beech trees to the line of hills.
Each window framed a distinct and lovely landscape, with
fields, hedges, wood, valley, hills and distant peaks complete.

The massive front door, so seldom used, hid in a deep
stone porch covered with honeysuckle, in the centre of the
building. It led into a stone-flagged hall, which was lighted
by narrow windows, through which the golden motes
danced in straight lines, slanting to the floor. On one side a
door led to the kitchen, the living-room of the farm, and on
the other sides, doors led to the parlour, the south parlour
and the stone chamber. The parlours were gay with old
gilded wallpapers and in them were the soft tinkly piano
which only Susan played, a Sheraton bureau, a 'what-not'
with rows of little ornaments, old sofas and chairs draped in
antimacassars and stiff chintz, and great oak chests with pale
panelling, with intricate wreaths of flower and leaf, and
carved letters, w.m. 1644, w.g. 1796. Inside these were
wedding dresses, in faded silks, falling to pieces, fichus in net
and hard lace, fringes and flounces, babies' long clothes,
funeral cards, and packets of letters in strange crabbed
writing, crossing and recrossing.

The stone chamber was a store room for seeds and cow
medicine, for books on farriery and breeding. An old
bureau stood in one corner, with a stool in front of it. Nobody came here, the windows were curtainless, and the
floor was bare. Roses pushed against the window and almost
screened it, so that the room was dim.

The kitchen was the heart of the house, a large low-ceil-
inged room full of doors and windows and old oak, and

people going to and fro. Along two sides were oak dressers, with shining brasses and beeswaxed sides, and drawers with their own distinctive names, apron drawer, rag drawer, sewing drawer, book drawer, duster drawer and bit drawer, child's drawer and girl's drawer, towel drawer and writing drawer. A row of shelves, with a dinner service painted with bright trees and birds, and lustre mugs and buff jugs of satyrs and fauns, hung over one dresser, and a row of graduated dish-covers over the other, each one reflecting the bright fire opposite.

In the corner by the fireplace stood a settle with its panelled back covered and padded, and its seat a bed of blue and white check cushions. This was reserved for the farmer, and only his personal friends were invited to sit on it. Under the ceiling ran a corner shelf laden with brass and copper preserving-pans, brass saucepans, and copper tankards, of great age, but all bright and shining. The mantelpiece, too, was full of brass candlesticks, square and round, and gleaming mugs and measures.

There was a copper warming-pan, used every night in the winter, and a row of horses' head ornaments, moons and sun of brass, tinkling bells, and plated brushes, kept dry and clean. There were whips and guns, lanterns and a pistol, an old blunderbuss and a pole-axe.

Everything shone, everything held a tiny red flame in its heart, but the shiniest, most important thing was the grandfather clock which ticked solemnly in its corner, where it had stood for two hundred years, joining in every conversation, interrupting with a loud whirr when it was displeased, holding its breath when the house was quiet, listening, listening to things long forgotten.

A door from the kitchen led through a stone arched passage to the pantry and dairy with its stone benches round the walls and pans of milk set out for cream, a large, cold, airy room, with big windows at a corner round which the gales screamed in winter. Just outside the back door, a broad wall built on the rock held the milk-cans, put upside down

to sweeten in the wind, which sometimes caught them and
threw them down the hill to the beech wood. The water
troughs were near, great stone troughs sunk in the rock, fed
by an ever-running spring, with a background of ferns.

A wing started out at one side and wandered along em-
bracing the old brewing-house, another kitchen, a barn, and
a bed-chamber up a ladder and through a trap-door, for an
odd labourer. At right angles to this again, so that it enclosed a courtyard, was a line of farm buildings, rows of
stone-coloured doors, steps running up the outside walls to
lofts which had forgotten the reason of their existence. Once
Susan, exploring, discovered a spinet, covered with dust,
half hidden in some straw in one of these chambers. She
played a tune and the sweet cracked notes tinkled to the
rats, which stopped shuffling for a moment among the
worm-eaten boxes and bales of straw. In another loft she
found a store of books, shut up in a chest, herbal books,
bound magazines of 1840, sermons, hymns, and tracts,
which she read for many a day.

The stables, cart-sheds, and barn were in this wing, built
along a side of the foundation rock, with great walls and
heavy doors, to stand the wildest storm. The main cow-
houses were on the open ground to the east, in a more
sheltered position.

A grass plot, with a monkey tree in the middle, stretched
up to the front windows of the house, close to the walls like a
green mat, for Tom Garland delighted to keep it even and
clipped like the pony's coat. It was bounded by a rounded
sandstone wall, so densely covered with ferns and stonecrop
that the horses nibbled it when they were left alone for a
minute in the waiting cart, and had to be driven off. Beyond
the broad gravelled road which joined the cobbled yard and
old buildings to the newer barns and the main gate was a
stretch of lawn with a grindstone in the middle and a wild
flower garden at the edge. Daffodils, cowslips, and snow-
drops made it their home. It ended abruptly in a steep drop,
so that the ground was level with the tops of the trees in the

orchard, and Becky had either to go round by the gates or climb down the rough steps projecting in the bounding wall.

This lawn too was surrounded by a low wall, bright with ferns and gilliflowers, with clumps of white rock hanging down like snow in spring. At a corner of the house stood a group of yew trees, gloomy, black, jewelled with scarlet berries, and walled off from the horses who might eat of the leaves and die.

Down a flagged path, past the yew trees and rose beds, stood the pig-cotes, which were older than the house itself. Their thick stone walls were smothered in roses and honeysuckle, which covered the back in a wild tangle, unpruned and rioting. The sloping roof, with its large flat stones, was embossed with giant house-leek, great cushions of the juicy rosettes, with starry red flowers, planted in ancient days for inflammations and sores, and still used by the farmer. The cotes had a fern-covered wall a yard thick round their paved court, and beyond was a little enclosed garden – the pig-cote garden – where the pigs played sometimes. Lilacs and currants grew thick round the edge, rats from the old walls scurried in and out of the heavy grass. Over all, a benign mother, hung an enormous elder tree, dropping her delicate petals in the row of little stone troughs, decking the grass in the enclosure, and, in autumn, pouring her berries in the brown baskets of Dan and Becky, ready for the purple wine-making.

The pigs were great friends of Susan's, and she spent many days on the roof, playing house among the clumps of house-leek, or walking round the broad wall, talking to the grunters, listening to their answering snorts as she threw down windfalls and acorns. The sows were detestable, with their sharp cruel little eyes, but the piglets were like children, their glances soft and curious. They recognized her voice and cried shrilly when she called them and rattled the long-handled copper bowl on the stone trough outside their outer door.

All the buildings were whitewashed, the dairy, pantry, kitchens and outhouses, the stables, barns and cow-houses. Only the old hay chambers were left, silent, listening, with their cumber of past days, worm-eaten and heavy, with a strange, curiously exciting smell, parts of spinning-wheels, giant presses, cheese-stones, a broken cradle, and a medley of old boxes.

In one of the bedrooms, the apple chamber, apples were stored for the winter; another, with a north window, had once been the cheese room. Now that the railway ran through the valley most of the milk was sent to a town, except a little which was kept for butter, and the cheese chamber was no longer stored with the great round cheeses which had left their round marks on its stone floor. There was the lad's chamber, which had belonged to generations of servant men, and the wench's chamber, now renamed the girl's room, where Becky slept. There was the old chamber with its crooked floor and heavy beams which Joshua occupied, and the attic, where Susan looked down on the outside world from her tower in the tree-tops.

Mr and Mrs Garland had a double-bedded room called the oak chamber, which contained two enormous four-posters with pink and blue diapered linen hangings which never wore out. It was the birth and death room. In that room Susan was born, and her father was born too. Her grandfather and great-grandfather had all come into the world in that same square chamber with its vision of orchard and garden, dipping valley and shining river, and black everlasting woods massed against the sky. There many old men and women had died, and young ones too, but one man had fallen asleep in the field among the mowing grass, and one had slipped from life in the saddle as he rode up the hill on his mare. When his time came, Tom Garland too would lie in a last sleep in that room.

One little room was Susan's in the winter when she came down from the freezing attic to a fire and curtains. It was shut away from the others, the little chamber down a little stair, and through double doors, exactly underneath her attic, but sheltered and warm.

The best room was the parlour bedroom, and into it Susan tiptoed whenever the door was left unlocked. It was in a gable at the end of the house, and had wide windows on two sides, one framing the Dark Wood, the orchards, the river and the hills, the other looking towards the homely stack-yard, the plough field, the wild steep larch wood, the beech wood, Arrow Head, and the pastures. But Susan did not come to see these, nor the rose trees which nodded and tapped at the window from spring to November. She came to peep at the treasures that were kept there.

Inlaid work-boxes and fitted dressing-boxes stood on the high chests of drawers between a pair of wig-stands, and slender pewter candlesticks. Inside them were reels of silk with tasselled ends, ivory brooches, jet bracelets, a blue leather pincushion with worn silk edges, a Valentine, a gold pencil, a pen-wiper with a black velvet dog and puppy lying on the top, a locket with a dove holding an olive branch, chains of silver with pink and grey stones inlet, scissors with gilt handles, an ivory needle-case, a mosaic cross, and clusters of little curls wrapped up in tissue paper.

Susan never tired of looking at these things. It was the treat she chose for her birthday, her reward for picking many pounds of blackberries.

A Queen Anne table stood at the bottom of the wide bed with its silk and velvet patchwork quilt, and on it lay a pair of fine steel candle-snuffers. A carved square stool, also covered with patchwork, stood in front of the dressing-table, and Susan sat there looking at herself, staring at her black eyes and wishing they were blue, touching her short dark hair and longing for golden curls. In the dressing-table she had once found a secret drawer, which gave her intense satisfaction. She wrote on a slip of paper, 'Susan Garland

wrote this. Windystone Hall Farm. Aged nine.' She shut it
up in the drawer for future ages to find, perhaps a little
Susan in another hundred years, who would give a thought
to the dead and gone Susan Garland, as she herself thought
of the children who had once played there. But a few days
later her mother opened the drawer and burnt the paper, so
it wasn't a secret drawer after all.

She wished she could sleep once in the high oak bed,
under the many-coloured quilt with its hexagons of moss-
like velvet and flower-petal silk. She fingered the patterns,
bits of her mother's wedding dress, finery sent by an aunt,
pieces collected for years before she was born, 'or even
thought of', Margaret had said. She had slept in one of the
drawers of the mahogany chest when she was a baby. No
cradle was thought necessary, and she had lain secure on a
blanket in the drawer which was placed on two chairs next
to her mother's bed in the other room. She wished she could
remember it, and she opened the drawer to peep inside.

In it lay a little white plush bonnet, her own. Was there a
baby's head inside with straight black hair, and tiny limbs
kicking the wooden walls?

Hark! Hark! Who spoke then?

It was the room whispering urgently, trying to tell her
something. She stood still, the waves of intense feeling swept
across her, as if hands stroked her head and a cloak wrapped
her round. Then it stopped. A rose tapped on the window,
and life went on. There was no one there, except the butterflies which sat sunning themselves on the broad white
window-sill, before they hid for the winter in corners of the
room. The first tortoiseshells always appeared in the parlour
bedroom in the spring – they were the only guests who were
allowed in, except distinguished visitors, such as the Squire,
or Miss Dickory, Susan's godmother.

Every week Mrs Garland put the warming-pan between
the sheets to keep it in airing, and every day she opened the
windows to let in the sunshine. The room was her pride, a
little private chapel, where she was the priest.

Margaret Garland was a round-cheeked, apple-faced woman, with brown hair taken straight back from her low, beautiful forehead. She was very different from her pale, thin-faced little daughter. People said they did not know where Susan got her ill-looks, the child was all eyes. It certainly was not from hearty Tom Garland with his blue eyes and big open face. His cheeks were ruddy and smooth, he towered a good-looking giant over his elfish daughter, who was no use to him on the farm. Margaret Garland said Susan took after her Aunt Elizabeth who died when she was a girl. It was terrible to look like someone who was dead, thought Susan, and she whistled and climbed trees to make herself a boy.

Margaret's eyes were grave, but when she laughed a little light shone out of them, so that Susan thought there must be a candle somewhere behind. She had even seen it when her mother leaned with the candlestick in her hand to kiss her in bed, a little flame on a white candle, only as big as a pin's head. There was a candle in Susan's eyes, too, which burned ardently when she ran down the fields to search for treasure, or read *Robinson Crusoe* by the kitchen fire, but she seldom looked at her own face, for her looking-glass was too high up on the top of the chest of drawers, and the glass was old and spotted with mouldy stars.

Mrs Garland was too busy to give much time to Susan, except to instruct her in religion. She was as intent on her house as a bird on its nest building.

Everything was scrubbed and rubbed, washed and cleaned, and no one could make even a dirty fingermark without being found out.

Farmer Garland could not abide the scrubbing and rubbing, and when things were at their worst he retired to his workshop up a stone stairway, and locked himself in with half-made hen-coops and besoms. Susan was drawn into the fray to dust and polish, to fetch and carry, to clean the brass and wash the cans, but she, too, escaped whenever she could, to the fields and garden in the summer, where she hid among the currant bushes, or to the dark warm barns in the winter. She stayed her hunger with cow cake and pieces of swedes, and crunched the indian corn, but at last she had to go home, compelled by darkness and rats and a keen appetite. Her ears were boxed and she was given a bowl of bread and milk for supper instead of bread and dripping or hot roast potatoes and butter, and sent to bed without a candle.

She sobbed, but when she said her prayers she asked for God's forgiveness and lay down happy. That was the best of prayers, she could sin quite a lot in the day, knowing that when she prayed she would be forgiven. She heard that at church, where she prayed every Sunday, 'We have done those things which we ought not to have done, and there is no health in us.' Whether she had been good or bad she prayed the same words, and got the same forgiveness.

CHAPTER 3

Idols

EVERY Sunday Mrs Garland and Susan hurried down the hill and along the white road to church, listening to the clanging bells, which bade them be quick. Ting tong, ting tong, they went, echoing against the hills, now clear, now so faint, as the rush of the river and the curves of the road carried away the sound, that Susan thought they had stopped. Mrs Garland walked, but Susan ran at a jog-trot, dropping behind and then catching up, until she had a stitch in her side, for no one could keep up with her mother when she was late for church. They raced along by the lovely river and had no time to look at flowers or birds, at the tree-creeper running up the sycamore tree, and the kingfisher flashing under the alders. Shafts of sunlight fell on their faces, but they panted on. They passed the weir and the ivy-covered mill-house with never a glance at the purling water.

The slow bell began, tong, tong, tong, and Susan's stitch nearly made her cry; but being late was worse, with the staring congregation saying:

'There go Mrs Garland and Susan, late again. I should think shame if I was them.'

Yet it was the same every Sunday, for one reason or another. Susan forgot her prayer-book, Mrs Garland turned back to remind Becky to baste the sirloin, Susan tumbled and dirtied her silk gloves, Mrs Garland stopped behind to make a pudding.

On this Sunday, just as they crossed the bridge over the river and climbed the steep hill to the church the bell stopped. They followed after the choir and in the confusion and rustle of standing up they slipped into their seats near the front, breathless and scarlet, Mrs Garland's velvet bonnet tilted on one side, Susan's hat shamelessly perched on the back of her head. It might have been worse; sometimes they were at the Psalms when they entered.

Susan knelt down on the red baize hassock beside her mother with her eyes just peeping over the edge of the old pew. She could see the altar and the flowers, and the bright light of God shining on the candlesticks. He was everywhere, He filled the church, but especially the chancel, where He hovered like an invisible angel, all misty with shining edges, the sun behind the cloud, listening to the prayers.

She shut her eyes and joined fervently in the service. Even the vicar had noticed Susan Garland in church. She never turned round, she sang all the hymns, she fixed her eyes on him during the sermon in a disquieting way, as if she searched his soul. But today her attention wandered, some wonderful smell on a lady's dress disturbed her, a heavy, rich, intoxicating scent, unlike anything in the garden, not lavender, or roses, honeysuckle, or violets. She opened her eyes a crack, hoping God would not mind. It came from behind, so she could not find out its source.

By her side was her mother's best silk umbrella, with its handle an ivory dog's head, tiny eyes, and little straight-back ears, its minute dog collar and chain winding round the slim neck. Susan stroked it with one finger and softly rubbed it against her cheek. So clean, so cold, and all made of ivory. Africa, green parrots, crocodiles, tigers, black men with assegais hunting the great-eared monstrous elephants pounding through the jungle on legs like beech trunks. And then to be just a little umbrella in church, listening to 'Our Father, which art in heaven'.

Her mother nudged her and she shut her eyes again and prayed hard. Her conscience began to prick, she was not quite sure of so much forgiveness.

'Thou shalt have none other gods but me,' said the vicar. 'Lord, have mercy upon us,' began the congregation. A god was an idol, made of wood or stone. Her doll must be an idol, her legless wooden doll. A disconcerting thought which she pushed into the background.

'Thou shalt not make to thyself any graven image.' There it was again; she loved Rose better than anything, and she was a graven image.

'Thou shalt not take the Name of the Lord thy God in vain,' and only that morning she had said, 'Goodness gracious', which Becky said was swearing God be gracious. Nobody swore at Windystone, only her father sometimes said 'Dang' when he was very angry. She began to feel miserable.

'Remember that thou keep holy the Sabbath Day.' Of course the man-servant and maid-servant had to milk the cows and fodder the horses, that was necessary work. Susan had early learned the distinction. Nobody ever read a newspaper or whistled a tune, except hymns, at Windystone on Sundays. For a moment she felt superior.

'Honour thy father and thy mother.' She was safe again.

'Thou shalt do no murder.' Oh, horrible word, haunting word! Charles Peace and Jack the Ripper! Why was everyone so calm when they said it? It struck terror in her heart.

'Thou shalt not commit adultery.'

That meant kissing anyone with a moustache. Never again should the miller kiss her when she called at the mill with her father.

'Thou shalt not steal.'

Susan's conscience was getting out of control, swelling up into her throat till she thought she would be sick.

She had stolen a lucky-bag, long ago, from the little shop at Raddle, when she waited and waited and nobody came. She never had a penny to spend, and there the paper bag lay, 'Monster Lucky Bag', with some others in a pile on the counter, asking her to open it.

She hid it under her pinafore and when cross Old Mother Siddal at last came in, wiping the soap-suds off her hands, she had innocently asked for the pound of rice her mother wanted.

Her face went so red she was afraid that Old Mother Siddal would guess and send her off to prison at once. But for once she smiled a vinegary smile at Susan and asked the price of eggs at Windystone.

She felt sorry she had deceived the old woman, but it was too late, and she hurried off to open the surprise bag, feeling uncomfortable and hot. Everybody seemed to look at her that day.

When Susan passed the policeman, whom she very seldom saw, for he had three villages to look after, he stared back at her wide, frightened eyes, and she thought he must know. She had opened the bag in the field by the wood and found a riddle, a spinning-top and a box of lemon kali. But she had no heart to touch the things and burnt them when she got home. She thought God had forgiven her, but evidently He hadn't, although she had prayed, and had even hidden a penny in the shop some weeks later when she had one. Tears came into Susan's eyes and began to trickle down her face. She dare not wipe them away, and they fell plop! on her prayer-book. She quickly rubbed her gloved finger over them, but her mother had seen.

'What's the matter, Susan?' she whispered.

Susan did not reply.

'Have you a pain, my dear?'

Susan nodded, the pain was in her heart.

Mrs Garland slipped half a chlorodyne lozenge from her bag into Susan's hand, and the child sucked it with a consciousness of sin and misery.

In the sermon she felt better; it was about the Prodigal Son. The vicar told the old story, but Susan's thoughts embellished it and raced all round it like a puppy running up and down the field as his master plods faithfully on the footpath. She always liked the son, he had such an adventurous life. But husks were not nice, she felt sorry for him then. She had tasted bran mash and found it quite delicious, but the husks were dry and choked her as they must have choked the young man.

Then he had returned to his father, wondering if he would be at home. But the old man had seen him a long way off and waved his handkerchief, and had run down by the orchard, through the field with the brambles and gorse bushes, unheeding the prickles, till he met him at the corner of the lane, where the holly bush stood guard. He flung his arms round his son and kissed and hugged him. The servants had killed the fatted calf, stuffed it with forcemeat, thyme and parsley from the garden, and served it with thick gravy. What a feast! How the young man had enjoyed it after the husks! And the ring on his finger too! Once Susan had worn a ring; it was from a cracker, a brass one her mother said, but she was sure it was gold because there was a ruby in it. But the ring stuck! Oh, the horrible feeling! She got quite hot as she thought of how she tried to pull it off, and Becky had said it would have to be cut off; she knew someone who had her finger cut off to remove a stuck ring. She pulled and pulled till the ruby fell out, but the ring would not move, and her finger became red and swollen.

Susan's horrified eyes gazed at the clergyman.

Her mother held her hand in the cold water trough, in the icy water, and wonderful, off came the ring. Now it lay in cotton wool, in a pill-box, with the stone fastened in with pincers, but nothing, nothing would induce her to wear a ring again. She hoped the Prodigal Son knew about the cold water trough.

What was he saying? 'Now to God the Father.' He had finished. Susan loved the hymn that followed, ' Rock of ages, cleft for me', and she sang with all her might, for she knew it by heart. Her eyes were fixed on the blues and purples in the stained-glass windows over the altar, but her thoughts were of a great rock in the middle of a raging sea, to which she clung with her fingers in a crack, like the picture of the lovely girl in the blue nightgown which came with the groceries at Christmas. She had asked her mother to have it framed, but it was still waiting for 'Some rainy day when it's fine'.

Slowly the congregation filed out of church, and the organ rolled and thundered. Susan could now look at the gentry and admire their haughty stares. She wondered why they had such big noses and thick hair. She listened to the swish, swish of their skirts as they walked in front of her up the aisle, and she sniffed at the lovely smells coming from their clothes. She found the exotic smell in the dress of a strange young lady with lips like roses, and eyes as bold as brass, staring round the church.

Susan sighed her admiration of this foreigner. Behind Sir Harry Vane sat two pews full of maids, demurely dressed in black, with small neat bonnets on their parted hair. They hurried out of church before the family, like a company of mice before a cat. Sir Harry Vane, as the Squire, the owner of many farms and most of the villages and land, had the right to turn round in church and to go up first at Holy Communion. Susan's glance never ventured higher than his gold watch-chain and seals.

There was Mrs Stone, the vicar's wife, in a dress of mauve silk which swept singing over the flat tombstones in the aisle, tombstones which Susan scarcely dared tread upon lest she should insult the dead. Little *ruches* trimmed the edge, like furry violets. Long jet earrings hung from her small pointed ears. In front of the bodice at the top of the row of purple buttons she wore a brooch, a twist of hair behind a glass, like a picture with a gold frame. Susan tried to peep round at it, but the cold eyes of Mrs Stone kept her in her place.

There were the girls from Dial Grange, with their hooked noses and long hair, thick as a horse's tail. They wore blue coats all alike, and each had a little gold brooch, with her initials in pearls, at her throat. They walked out with their governess, each carrying twin prayer and hymn-books in red morocco cases.

Then came Sir Harry's housekeeper, a stout comfortable

woman with a high bosom. She walked slowly and sedately as befitted her rank. The beads in her bonnet nodded and her silk crackled and shone. Susan and Mrs Garland walked down the hill among the graves with her. The little girl felt shy before such an important person and never spoke, but Mrs Garland chattered until they parted at the lodge gates.

There were whirlpools in the River Seale, and if you fell in you would go down, down, twisting in a circle, caught fast by the water, and your body would never be found. Susan never went near the edge, even to gather the purple foam of wild geraniums in the hot summer days, or the tall spikes of loose-strife in the spring. She looked at the glittering water from the dusty lane and kept away, for Becky said water attracts you like a tree draws lightning, or a red rag a bull.

Beauty spread its arms before her. The little waves rippled and danced with their leaf-boats sailing like the nautilus. Elms dipped their branches to kiss the water as it bubbled past, and threw their yellowing leaves across it like a shawl, but Susan kept her distance.

She dawdled along behind her mother, picking a fern, a scrap of scarlet-leaved robin-run-in-the-hedge, a piece of moss with drinking-cups for elves, stooping for a little stone which she rubbed on her stocking to see if the flecks were pure gold. All these she put in her capacious pocket, in the folds of her cashmere dress.

A robin stammered out his little note, and then trilled into a cascade of song, as he watched her from a stump. A brown bird sang like water dropping, twinkling into a bowl from a tap, or into the stone trough at the back door.

Flat clouds swam in the sky, and arrows of birds shot across. But Susan's mind was full of foreboding, she was still distressed about her sins, and felt that, like Abraham, she must make a sacrifice, but whereas Abraham was stopped at the last moment she saw no chance of escape.

She put away her prayer-book and Sunday gloves in the carved and wreathed bureau in the hall, and hung her best hat and coat in the wardrobe. Then she sat down between her father and mother at the big table in the kitchen. Tom Garland, in his best suit of broadcloth, his broad silk tie and gold and pearl tie-pin, sat at one end of the table, watching every movement, keeping an eye on Susan, and savouring the joint. He liked his food exactly and correctly done. The smoking sirloin of beef lay on a large willow-pattern dish in front of Mrs Garland. As she cut each slice Becky carried the plate to the stove, and added a large helping of potatoes, greens, and Yorkshire pudding from the black saucepans and dish, squatting on the hob like broody hens.

At the bottom of the table were seats for Becky and the old man Joshua. Dan sat at the dresser on a high stool, squeezed next to the whips and guns. He had a square of oil-cloth in front of him, and an ancient pewter salt-cellar, a two-pronged fork and a bone-handled knife with a pointed tip, on which he dexterously carried peas, gravy and all small things, with the abandon and skill of a juggler.

He sat staring at the lustre mugs and the satyrs on the jugs, waiting for his turn.

'Say Grace, Susan,' commanded Mrs Garland.

'For what we are going to receive the Lord make us truly thankful,' said Susan, shutting her eyes and holding up her two small hands over the table cloth.

'What sort of sermon did you have today, Margaret?' asked Tom, as he attacked his piled-up plate and helped himself to horse-radish sauce.

'A very good one, about the Prodigal Son,' answered Margaret. 'But what do you think? He told us again how poor he is, and what a poor living it is. And there was Mrs Stone in a beautiful mauve dress. He said he had only four hundred pounds a year, and the vicarage. That's all.'

'Eh! That's all, is it?' said Tom Garland with a dry laugh. 'That's all.'

Old Joshua, Dan, and Becky laughed too, and Susan joined in the merriment. Dan put down his knife and fork and guffawed so heartily he began to choke, and had to retire to the yard under Tom's displeased stare.

'I wish I had four hundred pounds a year coming in and all I had to do was to preach a sermon every Sunday,' said Tom.

'He does more than that,' Margaret rebuked him. 'He visits, you know, he goes to see the poor.'

'And the rich too,' said Tom coldly.

'Yes, he's going to dine at the Court today, Mrs Bunch told me.'

'How many pheasants and partridges does he get a year from the Squire, I wonder? How many bunches of grapes? Eh, those parsons, they're never content, they deserve to want.'

Old Joshua joined in. 'The Son of Man had not where to lay His head, and they grumble at four hundred pounds a year and a fine house free of rent, and all their coal found too!'

Susan sat thinking of her doll. She loved it very much, and she told it everything, but it was a creature of wood. 'Cast out every idol,' said a voice inside her.

Even the damson tart and cream did not raise her spirits.

'What's the matter, Susan? Where's your tongue? Count your stones and see who you'll marry.'

'Tinker, tailor, soldier, sailor, rich-man, poor-man, beggar-man.'

'A beggar-man,' said Susan, so dolefully they all laughed, and she thought of the old man who came to the door with a sack on his back for rabbit skins. It wasn't a cheerful prospect and she felt more unhappy than ever.

When Becky was washing up, and Margaret had gone in the parlour with *Sunday at Home*, and Tom had lain down on the settle for his Sunday nap beside the hot fire, Susan crept quietly to the pantry where the doll lay in a wooden toy box, under the stone bench. She knelt on the sanded floor among the candles and jars of lard, and lifted it out.

It was dressed in flowered muslin, gathered round its thick neck, and fastened round the waist with a ribbon. It had neither legs nor arms, hair nor eyes, it was carved in one piece, with sightless eye-balls and open lips, but its head was smooth with the caress of hands and its cheeks were soft and sweet to the child's lips.

Susan examined it critically, as she sat on the cold floor. Yes, it must be an idol, it looked like one, it was far, far older than she was, for it was at Windystone Hall before she was born or even her father was born. It was no ordinary doll, like Laura, waxen and golden-haired, or Rosamund who could open and shut her eyes. They had hands and feet but no understanding. Rose knew everything, she knew now what was in Susan's thoughts, and she looked at her piti-fully with her blind all-seeing eyes.

She must go, she must either be drowned or burned. Burning was too horrible, Susan could not bear the thought of it. It was like the Christian martyrs, and suppose Rose cried out in the flames? Drowning was best.

She kissed the dark wooden face and held her tightly against her breast, with her cheek against the top of the smooth round head. She sidled through the back door to the water-troughs. She undressed her, for Susan was econo-mical, and prayed a little prayer. Then she plunged her down into the water.

Like a live thing Rose sprang up and lay floating, a brown Ophelia among the oval damson leaves and the yellow elm in the green reflection of the ferns. Sunlight dappled her wet face with golden flecks. Never had Rose looked so alluring. Was this Abraham's miracle? No, she was made of wood, Susan had forgotten that, and she tenderly lifted her out and dried her on her petticoat.

'Susan, Susan,' cried a voice from the apple chamber. 'Whatever are you doing at the water-trough? Get up at once, do you hear? And in your Sunday dress, too. You mustn't play with your doll on Sundays,' and her mother withdrew her head.

Susan walked off down the flagged path to the pig-cote and leaned against the wall. She would have to bury Rose. It was quite the best thing to do, and then she wouldn't be really gone. 'I can't worship her, yet I shall always know where she is. Perhaps some day a man will dig her up, and think she was buried by the Romans.'

This cheered her so much she began to sing, 'There is a happy land, far, far away,' as she skipped into the kitchen for a knife.

Under a great ash tree which stood solitary in the middle of Whitewell field, spreading out its branches in a roof under which all the cattle could shelter at the same time, Susan dug the grave. She removed little patches of earth and scrabbled with her fingers among the roots until she had a hole big enough. Ants ran by, carrying tiny sticks, and a pair of wood-pigeons moaned softly, oblivious of the small figure struggling so far beneath their leafy floor. Jays screamed on Arrow Head, and a magpie flew out of Druid's Wood and flirted his tail on the oak trees bordering the field.

Susan ran back for a bunch of clean-smelling camomile which grew in silvery tuffets under the yew trees. She lined the grave with this, and laid Rose with her face upwards to the sky. She shut her eyes and put her hands together, as she crouched on her heels. 'Please God help me not to worship idols, and take care of Rose', she prayed, and then she covered up the wooden figure with the sod.

Her conscience was satisfied and pride filled her. She felt she had done rather a noble self-sacrificing deed. But when night came and she lay in her chamber alone, tossing under the heavy quilt, she could not sleep. She stared out at the stars among the branches of the elm tree, and the Great Bear hanging over the quiet fields. A shooting star fled across the sky, and faded out near the branches of the ash tree. It was the soul of someone who had died, going to God.

A fox barked in the woods and Roger rattled his chain. A light danced across the path, and long beams streamed over the grass. It was Joshua going to see the sick cow in the byre. A rabbit squealed in the misty copse and then was silent. An owl hooted suddenly overhead and a noiseless shadow drifted by. Susan thought of Rose lying out in the field with hedgehogs walking over her grave, and perhaps worms crawling on her face. It was too much, a big tear ran down her cheek, and then another and another.

A mouse scrit-scratched in a corner of the room and scampered across with horribly loud feet. Susan longed for the feel of that smooth head to protect her. Rose was a weapon as well as a companion, she had frightened away many a venturesome mouse by bumping her head on the floor. Wearied out she fell asleep, and only awoke when Becky shook her.

It was Monday morning, and seven o'clock, a pearl of a day, an opalescent creamy autumn morning. For a moment something worried her as she sat up in bed, and then the thought rushed out from behind the screen of warmth and comfort. Rose was buried under the ash tree.

She washed and dressed quickly, from her calico chemise and soft grey stays to her white garibaldi, blue skirt and clean pinafore. Mrs Garland was pouring out tea from the big brown teapot as she entered the kitchen. She took a slice of toast and dripping and sat down to the table.

Tom Garland, Joshua, and Dan came to the back door with cans of foaming milk and slung them on the iron pole over the water-troughs to cool. The house was full of the sounds of morning: the rattle of the chains, the trot-trot of the horse's hoofs along the drive as he went to the stable to be harnessed, the slithering clatter as he was backed into the loading place, waiting for the milk-churns, the wheeling of churns, Roger's excited barks as he ran up and down, the banging of doors, and the stamping of many feet.

'Come along, Susan, and stir the milk,' called Tom, as he walked through the house and went out at the front. Dan and Joshua had gone back to the cow-house for more milk, whilst Becky ran to and fro helping everyone.

Susan snatched a cup from the table as she went out, and dipped it in a can. It came out white with a thick cream, covered with a froth which gave her a milk moustache. She sipped as she stirred with the hazel stick first one and then another of the row of cans hanging deeply in the water of the troughs. The largest trough was used for drinking purposes only. Into this a spring sent its clear icy water, jutting out from the cool earth, gurgling, crystal, never dry in the worst droughts, and from it the water overflowed through holes cut in the thick stone to the series of milk-troughs.

When the milk was cool and Dan had swallowed a basin of scalding tea and eaten a round of toast, the cans were all lifted from the troughs and carried round the house to the cobbled yard for measuring. This was Susan's chance, and she ran off down the path, past rose bushes and pear trees, to Whitewell.

'Are you there, Rose?' she called anxiously, as she went across the broad field. Rabbits sat up and watched her, nibbled a blade of grass and sat up again, deeply interested. She clapped her hands, and they ran on a few steps. Jays quarrelled, thrushes and blackbirds fluted in the woods all round.

'Are you there, Rose?' she called again. 'There, Rose,' answered the echo. She started; she never knew an echo lived in the field. One dwelt at the Wishing Gate, under the biggest beeches in the world. It was a friend of Susan's, a comforter in loneliness, a mystery she had never solved, which she accepted as she accepted life and death, the stars and springtime. Many hours had she spent standing by the gate calling across the field with her face towards the big cart-shed, calling to see if it would say anything different. Three words at a time was all it would say, so she split up her sentences and tried to catch it tripping.

'Hello, Echo,' she began.

'Lo, Echo,' replied the echo.

'How are you?' asked Susan.

'How are you?' answered the echo.

So the conversation went on and she delighted to bring a stranger to be amazed at its clarity, as it sang high and low, soft and loud, from the merest whisper to a shout.

Now here was a sister echo, not so talkative, but quite de-

lightful. Certainly Rose had great power. She ran to the tree
and hastily removed the soil. There lay Rose, faintly smiling,
calm and mysterious, none the worse for her burial. She rubbed her with her pinafore and examined her face tenderly.
Then she kissed her and held her against her thin chest.

'I won't do what God wants,' she cried. 'I won't, Rose.'
Seven rooks flapped across the golden sky, a lucky number.
Birds sang wildly, rapturously, and the sun streamed across
the misty valleys and laid long fingers on Susan's head. Her
child conscience slept again, she laughed and skipped along
the broad path, through the tall stile, under the yews and
damson trees to the house.

'Susan, where have you been? Your breakfast is all cold.
Come and write the milk tickets at once. Dan is ready, and
the milk is scyed.'

Susan put her doll in the pantry box, climbed on a chair
and lifted down the box of milk notes and torn envelopes
from the high shelf of the tallboy. She took out a slip of
paper for each churn and wrote the number of gallons.
Becky put them in the little cups in the lids, and clamped the
bright outer lids with their polished brass plates. Dan and
Joshua came shouting and stamping down the cobbles, and,
seizing the churns, rolled them along on their rims, down the
narrow paved path to the loading place and into the cart.

Then Dan jumped in after them, cracked his whip, and
away he went, down the fields and tree-lined lanes, all
shining with gossamer, white in the mist, brushing his cap
against the nut trees and beeches, catching the wheels on
the arcs of reddening brambles and late blackberries.

It was the most romantic moment of the day, and Susan
and her father stood on the high bank watching the cart get
smaller and smaller as it rumbled with tossing churns down
the rough stony path in the distance.

'He drives a bit random,' said Tom, shaking his head.
'He needn't go in all that bluster, he's plenty of time,' and
they turned again to their disturbed breakfasts and Susan
got ready for school.

CHAPTER 4

School

WHEN Susan Garland was seven years old her mother sent her to the village school near Dangle, four miles away, for education was a serious problem in the out-of-the-way farms. It was a good way for the child to go alone, but Mrs Garland prayed long and earnestly for protection, and then left Susan in God's charge.

Susan was delighted, for she knew no children; the farm was too remote from others, except beautiful Oak Meadow Farm where old Mr and Mrs Wolff lived with their middle-aged daughter, Mary. So Susan had never a friend except the farm men and Becky. Margaret was glad she would mix with others, for the child was fanciful, and too fond of talking to herself and imaginary people. Her mind was full of fairies, goblins, and grown-up religious talk which she had overheard in the kitchen at home.

She had been taught to read, she was familiar with the Bible, and had read *Pilgrim's Progress*, the unabridged *Robinson Crusoe*, complete with the sermons, *Aesop's Fables*, and many religious stories and poems with morals attached. She was quick at figures and she had already made a sampler with cross-stitch men and trees. Susan looked forward to being someone of importance, when her mother took her to see the headmistress, but her hopes were soon dashed to the ground. Mrs Garland had found in an oak chest a dress which had belonged to a girl of a bygone age. It lay among blue silk-fringed crinolines and soft coloured Paisley shawls: a brown checked woollen frock with *ruches* of cut material trimming the tight bodice, and edging the high neck and the flounced skirt. It was buttoned from chin to foot with large cream bone buttons with steel centres. It was a godsend to Mrs Garland, warm as a blanket, strong as a horse-cloth, and thick. With a little alteration it made a new frock. Susan protested in vain, she wept, she hated its ugliness and the horrible buttons. So, a quaint old-fashioned little figure, her feet peeping out of the bottom frill which went nearly to her ankles, her chin almost lost in the top, she went for her first day at school.

Her short hair was strained back from her forehead and threaded through a round black comb which encircled her head like a coronet, with the hairs sticking up in a fringe at the back, 'being trained'.

She kept near her mother whilst she explained her hopes and fears for Susan to the sharp-eyed, thin-faced head-mistress, and watched with alarm the horde of children playing round the big door. Then Mrs Garland smiled be-nignly at all the little ruffians, kissed Susan 'God bless you, child,' and left her.

The village children laughed and pointed at her.

'What's your name?' they shouted.

'Susanna Catherine Mary Garland,' replied Susan, with her dark eyes wide and startled.

'What's your father?' they sang, swaying and swinging in a row, and pushing against her.

'I don't know,' said Susan, hesitating. It was the first time she had thought of this. In her little world there were no trades.

'Where do you come from?' they jeered, louder and louder, as they rocked with laughter at her simplicity.

Susan was on safe ground now. Had she not written it on the milk tickets each morning?

'From Windystone Hall, near Mellow,' she replied with a shy pride, as she thought of her domain, the wide fields and woods, the rambling house and buildings, and com-pared it with the tiny rose-filled gardens and thatched cottages of the village.

'Windy stone, rain stone, who went down the lane alone?'

mocked a wit, and the children shook back their hair and yelled with glee.

'Aye. What a figure of fun. Where did you get that frock?' they gibed.

She had loathed her dress, but now she held it tightly with one hand. It came from her own home, and was part of her. She had been called 'a figure of fun'. She stood with her back against the wall and a crowd of jeering girls jostled her. One pulled her hair with a mischievous tug, one opened her satchel and looked at her sandwiches, and one, the most shameless, put her tongue out at her. A little boy her own age ran up rudely and kissed her. He rushed away screaming with laughter, and Susan took out her handkerchief and rubbed her cheek as the cries and jibes rose higher. She stood like a frightened rabbit, her face white, her eyes big with horror. 'Mother,' she whispered to her heart, and the school bell rang.

The rabble dropped away and lined up in the playground. Susan went to the end of the row and followed them into a large room with pictures on the painted wall of Daniel in the lion's den, and a cocoa tree in flower. The lessons passed over her head. She could neither understand the strange accent and high voice of the town-bred teacher, nor grasp why she had to thread coloured strips through paper mats, with care and precision, and then pull them all out again. It was all working for nothing.

The sums were too easy, and the children round copied off her slate.

Books were given out for reading, and Susan's eye flitted rapidly down the pages. She was told not to turn over, so she sat dull and tired, waiting whilst the infants stumbled and fell over the little words. She was called on to read, and she read with expression as her mother had taught her. The children all turned round and stared, tittering and nudging one another. Susan's white cheeks became scarlet, her only wish was to be unnoticed. Covered with confusion she sat down, and her hair was sharply pulled from behind. She gave a short stifled cry, and Miss Hilda turned to her.

'What's the matter, Susan?' she asked kindly.

Susan whispered, 'Someone pulled my hair.'

Miss Hilda sent the naughty boy to a corner, but as he passed he hissed:

> '*Tell Tale Tit,*
> *Your tongue shall be slit*
> *And every dog in England*
> *Shall have a little bit.*'

Susan sat half stifled. Dan had once told her that he slit a starnel's tongue to make it talk. The story had sickened her, and now her tongue was to be slit. She determined to fight to death before they should get it from her.

Other children read in a monotonous sing-song, and so the weary time dragged on.

At playtime she went out with the others as a lamb to the slaughter. There were more questions and laughter, but Susan noticed some nice little girls whom she hadn't seen before standing in a group and smiling shyly at her. The horrible little boy came up. Susan stood, with lips firmly shut and her tongue safe inside her red mouth, ready for the struggle, but he only punched her arm and ran off crying, 'Tell Tale Tit'.

Then one of the girls asked Susan if she would like a drink, and took her to a tap in the wall with an iron mug hanging by a chain. The water was metallic and flat, it was the first tap water Susan had ever tasted, but she was grateful.

'Take no notice of them,' said her new friend. 'They don't mean anything,' and Susan was comforted. A weight was lifted off her heart, and as she walked into school again she felt she had been there for years. She could raise her head now and look at Elijah ascending into heaven in the chariot of fire, drawn by two prancing ponies, and the picture of a peacock hanging ready for a lesson, and the closed black stove which stood all alone in the middle of the floor with a pipe going out of its head. It was the strangest thing she had ever seen.

She was moved up, and took her place in the grammar class. Grammar was a nice-sounding word, she thought, like mother, or hammer, a comfortable homely word, but the lesson was incomprehensible. It was all about owls, or so it seemed to Susan. Miss Dahlia, who came from London, was treated with great respect as if she had come from heaven itself. Miss Dahlia began by informing the class that an owl was the name of anything.

'A table is an owl,' said Miss Dahlia, and nobody disagreed. Indeed nobody ever disputed anything Miss Dahlia said. The children vied with one another in calling everything an owl – chairs, horses, desks and elephants. They had heard it all before, and joined in when she told them of common and proper owls.

Now Susan, too, knew about owls. Her mind left the close stuffy room, with the smell of dust and children, and the high-pitched voice of Miss Dahlia. She saw the great tawny barn-owl which called over the house roof and hunted in the stack-yard and among the barns and cow-sheds. At evening, when the stars first appeared in the green sky, he sat in the fir tree at the corner of the garden. Susan had watched his dark shape against the starry sky. He sat on a branch just below Orion's belt, and cried to the great hunter in the sky. Then he spread his wings and flew noiselessly to the sycamore tree.

She lay in the attic with the moonlight pouring in at the uncurtained window, making a pattern of elm leaves on the beamed ceiling, whilst the owls hunted overhead crying like babies, and the mice cowered in their holes.

Once one flew through the window of the parlour bedroom which had been left open and forgotten. He broke a blue Wedgwood jug and swept a white-patterned bowl off the mantelpiece. Her father caught him the next morning as he sat sulkily on the old lavender wash-hand jug, his eyes blinking and his funny eyebrows upraised. What a mercy he had not broken that, her mother said, holding up her hands in consternation at the mess!

They put him in the summer-house. That was an exciting day for Susan. She felt as if he were a captive Golden Eagle who would carry off a lamb, when she looked at him through the little panes of glass, and he stared back at her.

They took him bread and milk and a dead mouse in the mouse-trap. But at night she heard his call Too-whoo-oo-oo and his mate answered from the wood. The calls grew more frequent, nearer, and she sat up in bed, listening, excited. She wondered if the wife had her round eyes glued to the window. Then the cries became faint and ceased, but the next morning there was no owl, only broken panes of glass.

Still she heard him cry Too-whoo-oo when an arm shook her, and a voice cried in her ear, 'Susan Garland. What did I say? Wake up, you naughty little girl.'

Susan awoke in a fright. Strange faces were round her, people were laughing, she wasn't in her own bed.

'Stand on the form,' said Miss Dahlia sternly, and Susan climbed up, disgraced utterly on her first day. She was tired, bewildered, and confused when the afternoon ended.

The mistress held up a pin. 'I must hear this pin drop before anyone goes home.' Everybody held their breath, and the shuffles of little heavy boots ceased. The pin dramatically dropped with a tiny tinkle. School was surprisingly over and Susan was free.

Her gloves were taken from her and her hat thrown in the road. She picked it up and dusted it, overwhelmed by the manners of rude little boys. If they came to her house she would set the dog on them she comforted herself. Her mother met her in the wood, but Susan was years older, secretive, puzzled by life, determined to escape from school at all costs.

The next day she played truant. She stayed in the wood, hiding, and crept home after a few hours with a tale of a holiday. She pretended to be ill, and was kept at home and dosed with camomile and wormwood tea. She doubled back when she got beyond the orchard and slipped upstairs to her bedroom, where the sympathetic Becky fed her like a fugitive Royalist. She hid in a barn all day, braving the rats and darkness, sitting on a stone step with her skirts drawn tightly round her, a little ghost with no friend. They began to watch her enter the Dark Wood, but still she eluded them. Her desire was to find a hollow oak in which she could live during school hours, but although she searched and searched the big trees, like a woodpecker seeking a home, she never found a hole large enough to shelter her.

But gradually she became used to school life. She made friends among the little girls, and adored Miss Jessie, as the custom was. The brown dress got shorter as she shot up, and at last it wore out with the rough treatment it received, and she was promoted to last year's Sunday frock.

So she learnt to sing-song like the other children, and to recite the Creed and the collects and Gray's *Elegy*. She spent sunny afternoons learning 'The Motherless Boy', 'The Blind Girl', and 'Casabianca'. She sewed little seams in pink cotton and blue, and knitted gloves and stockings. At playtime she danced round with other girls, singing:

> *There was a farmer had a dog,*
> *And his name was Bobby Bingo.*
> *B-i-n-g-o.*
> *B-i-n-g-o.*
> *B-i-n-g-o.*
> *And his name was Bobby Bingo.*

and

> *I wrote a letter to my love*
> *And on the way I lost it.*
> *One of you has picked it up,*
> *And put it in your pocket,*
> *It isn't you, it isn't you, it isn't you, it is you.*

and

> *Oats and beans and barley grows,*
> *Neither you nor anyone knows,*
> *Neither you nor anyone knows,*
> *Where oats and beans and barley grows.*

As the farmer sows his seed,
As he stands and takes his heed,
He stamps his foot and claps his hand,
And round he goes to view the land.
Waiting for a partner, waiting for a partner,
Waiting for a partner, so open the ring and take one in.
Now you're married you must obey,
You must be true in all you say,
You must be kind, you must be good,
And help your wife to chop the wood.

She played 'Here we come gathering nuts in May', and 'Oranges and Lemons', and 'I had a little Moppet'.

She was warned against going near the pretty mill pond, covered with water buttercups, for Jinny Green-teeth lived there, just under the bright green scum, and she dragged little children down to the bottom who so much as dipped a finger among her flowers.

She was told of the little boy who drank water from a trough at the side of the road, and swallowed a frog. It grew and grew in his inside, till he swelled like a balloon, and the frog hopped out of his mouth.

She actually saw the little girl who was squinting when the wind changed, and her eyes got stuck, a strange cross-eyed infant.

A dwarf went to school, a poor hunchbacked child who would never grow any bigger, but to Susan he was romantically associated with a princess in a glass coffin. She boasted of him at home and was proud to know him.

She learned to wear an oak leaf on Royal Oak Day, lest she should be beaten with stinging nettles.

She ran from the old witch, bent and muttering, who could put a spell over her with a glance of her evil eye, but she smiled and nodded to the poor idiot boy who walked along the roads singing a vague song and waving his arm in the air.

Every day she became happier, every season brought its games: whips and tops, and marbles, blood-alleys and alley-taws, skipping-ropes, and shuttlecocks and battledores, five

stones, hopscotch and hoops, but every night she had the
same anxious walk among boggarts and ghosties and giants
and dwarfs.

So her school education went on, but her true learning
was at home, in the fields and woods, or in the kitchen after
tea, when her mother recited 'The Wind and the Sun',
'John Gilpin' and ballads of Robin Hood and Dick Turpin,
and Susan read her fourfold library.

One evening she went out into the fields with her rope.
The sun had dipped behind the far-away hill and it was too
late to run up the fields to catch another glimpse of him.
How often she had caught another minute of his red light
and then another by racing up the steep hills after he had
set, and finding him again. So she had climbed till she could
go no higher, and watched his face slowly move below Boar
Ridge. Then down she ran, long legs leaping, arms outstretched and the cold air filled her blood and blew through
her body to the wraith inside.

But now indigo shadows had crept up the valley from the
river, up past the little hills, past the crag on which the farm
stood, to the highest peaks, and the mysterious warm dusk
filled the vast cup. From the fir trees came the cries of owls,
and late rooks flapped across the pale green sky.

Susan skipped slowly across the broad field path, smooth
and worn by the constant passing of men to the far barns.
The rope dropped from her fingers and dragged through the
grass. She stood very still, with her head thrown back,
searching the pale sky for the first star.

She could feel the earth moving, a great majestic motion,
the fields and farm, the woods and hills were sailing away
through that limpid sky. She held her breath in wonder, she
felt as if she floated up and up into that silvery dome above
her. Then she saw her first star, a pin-point deep in that sea
of space. She lost it and found it again. Then another came
out, and another, from nowhere. She stared at the roof of
the world, and behold, a star appeared. She began to count.
They were all round her, the green sky had become radiantly,

darkly blue, the trees were black, the earth flew like a great bird.

She counted till she was mazed, and a beam of light shone across the field from the house. It was the lamp in the kitchen. She turned and walked home.

In bed she lay counting, hundreds and hundreds, every night more hundreds till she slept. Each day she went on, more and more, but the number never ended. They were more than the stars. So she got her first glimpse of infinity.

CHAPTER 5

Serving-Men

THE earth will not yield her riches without labour in those hilly districts where the soil is so thin that the bare bones of the world stick out like the ribs in a worn body. The spade strikes rock when it drives deep in the soil, and, after a storm, the lanes are beds of mountain streams, with no foot-hold for the scrambling, sweating horses.

The air is fresh as a drink of spring water, cupped in the hand as it jets out of the earth in the fields and runs away to fill a stone trough. The grass is sweet and clean for the cattle, but the crops are light, they need constant care and the work is hard.

Years go by, some with increase, but more with decrease, in wealth. There are bad years which break the farmer's heart, times when Nature seems to oppose his every effort, and to thwart his will at every turn. Storms destroy the crops, late frosts kill the fruit, lightning strikes the cattle sheltering under the trees, long-continued rain spoils the hay and corn harvests, droughts burn up the fields, and disease lies in wait for the beasts.

There are accidents, too, on these precipitous hill-sides. A broken wall or a gap may mean death, and an open gate may bring mutilation. Cows lose their footing and fall down the rocky woods, a young colt gets kicked and spoilt by another horse, cattle stray and are poisoned by deadly weeds.

But with unwearying patience the farmer starts again; mending, doctoring, bringing life out of death, sowing and reaping, he struggles with Nature.

Such a man was Tom Garland. Born at Windystone, all

his days spent under the sky, he was as much a part of the hillside as the trees and grass. He knew when a storm was brewing and sent the men to shut up the young things which could not look after themselves. He could smell rain afar, and knew the movements of the winds. He could build a wall with the great blocks of rough sandstone so that it was firm to stand the buffets of the mighty gales, and evenly regular to the eye.

His animals were sleek and well fed, for they were always put first; no beast was kept waiting for its food and drink. His own movements were slow, his walk was that of a sailor who has to fight through the storms, his eyes were sailor's eyes, too, blue and fixed on far horizons.

He never hurried a beast, for he said, 'Dumb creatures don't always want to be in a swither and sweat like humans.' His eyes darkened and his underlip stuck out ominously when he found a horse in a lather, or a cow laboured and panting.

Joshua Taberner who helped him was an old farmer who had seen better days. He had been too simple, too trusting, too easy-going, so he had been cheated and robbed. Men had borrowed from him and never repaid, dealers had swindled him over sales, until he had to sell everything and leave his rose-bowered farm. Now he lived with relatives and friends, asking for nothing but a small wage and a bed-room. He preferred to stay at Windystone where he was in-dependent, and he spent most of his time there.

Susan greeted his clean rosy old face with a cry of happy welcome. His teeth had gone and his sunken mouth gave him a womanly look, a dimpled soft expression, which the child loved. He had a store of little jokes and old tales, and a fund of good humour and laughter. He sat next to Becky at the bottom of the table, below the big glass salt-cellar, and he amused her and Susan with his anecdotes, all of which he began by clearing his throat, twinkling his eyes and saying, 'I've heeard tell as how'.

He loved flowers and trees and all animals. He knew the

uses of herbs as well as Tom himself, and could make an excellent green salve for bruises, and tansy tea for Susan in the spring. He made an ointment for his own eyes from the white flowers of eyebright which Susan picked in the deserted quarries, and elder-flower tea for Becky's freckled face.

He was a good gardener, too, and he and Tom made the three-cornered kitchen garden a wealth of fruit and flowers. He helped Tom in the veterinary work, for he was more reliable than Dan.

But his hands trembled and each year he became more feeble. He walked along the fields Come-day, Go-day, gazing across the folds of the hills to where his own little farm with the roses and marigolds was now under the direction of a stranger. He was as slow as a funeral. Then there was his tongue which must be chattering all the time when Tom wanted peace and quietness. So after some months he went off for a visit to one of his daughters, a shrew who drove him back to the farm, which had missed him and welcomed him again.

There were other helpers who came with the seasons. Eli Bunting, the rat-catcher, visited them twice a year, and brought a load of excitement with him. Work was suspended when he walked through the stile by the big spiked gate into the yard, and stood waiting with his little terrier Jack at his heels for the frantic barking to bring someone out.

He opened his bag and held up three ferrets, the colour of old ivory. They shot their long flat heads sideways and stared with their pink eyes at the little crowd that gathered. Then he put them back again, solemnly protesting they had had no dinner for three days and were ravenous for rats and rabbits. He tied them up, and threw down the bag to squirm and wriggle on the grass.

Tom Garland got his double-barrelled gun, old Joshua and Dan took heavy sticks and off they went to the stack-yard and barns, where they waited whilst the pink-eyed beauties chased rats and rabbits out of staddles and piles of wood, from behind the rows of ladders and the golden haystacks and the corn-rick, and the great bins in the shadowy barns.

Sometimes Susan stood on a gate for safety, but Becky always kept out of the way.

'I can't abide a rat!' she said, shivering, as she drew her full gathered skirts round her hips. 'I wouldn't go near not if it was ever so.'

Eli brought his dinner in his pocket and ate it on the garden wall with a brimming mug of hot tea which Becky gave him. He admired the girl with her rosy cheeks and quick blushes, and she liked his fresh complexion, his nose beaked like an owl, and his gay, clear eyes, but he bantered until she returned to the house 'fair mad with him'.

Sometimes a ferret was lost and he waited till dusk. They fetched some spades from the barn and dug out the missing one, who was gorging at a blood feast in the earth. Sometimes it stayed away for days and Eli hung about waiting, but sometimes it never returned, and they knew that in the underground struggle the little tiger had been overcome.

Ralph Swingler, the mole-catcher, was an older man, a nomad, roaming over many counties. It was said he slept under the hedges, for he walked many miles each day and turned up at dawn, when the men were milking and the fields were bathed in mist. He wore a moleskin waistcoat and a round pork-pie moleskin cap on his straight black hair. His high boots, leather leggings, and bright green handkerchief added to his outlandish strange appearance, so that he looked like a man from foreign parts.

'The Moody-wap Man', as they called him, carried a bunch of knobbly iron traps and a half-moon spade with which he dug out the varmints. He walked over the ground and set the traps with cunning, both in fields and garden, for the moles were everywhere, spoiling the grass for the cattle with their red-brown hills, undermining the garden's vegetables and flowers.

The next day he returned to dig out the little soft-furred moody-waps with their long pig-like snouts, lying dead in the tracks. There was something very appealing in the pink hands and half-closed fingers of the little beasts, as they lay in a pile waiting for him to carry them away. Susan and her father leaned over them, touching the skins with a finger, pondering their silkiness, but despising them as fur – as well have a cap made of rat skin, they thought. Abel Fern, the hedger and ditcher, had made a weskit of moleskin from skins he cured himself, but nobody at Windystone would touch the stuff.

Every two months a tall grey-haired pedlar came to the door, bearing a basket of tinware on his head, bright nut-meg-graters, kettles and dishes, scissors and colanders. Besides this he had a pack on his back containing coloured ribbons and cottons, combs, tapes, and all the odds and ends of the truckster.

'The truckster's here, the truckster's here, missus,' cried Becky, running upstairs to the bedrooms, or outside to the brew-house to bring Margaret to look at his stock.

The two women stood in the doorway fingering the contents of his pack, and Margaret always bought things she didn't want for the sake of the old man. Becky fetched her worn leather purse and counted the pennies. She had no days off to go spending money in the villages, and here was her shop. She bargained for a new comb and a little looking-glass, a red ribbon – she was partial to red – and a bordered cotton handkerchief, which she intended to keep by her for her master's birthday.

Margaret made him a fresh brew of tea and spread slices of cold bacon on home-made bread for him to eat.

'And how's your wife?' she asked, 'and your children?' and as often as not she gave him a few apples or pears, or a jam pasty to take for his family, who were grown-up and married, if she had considered. But she was sorry for the old man, walking the country-side, in all weathers, rheumatism and all, over the hills and along the endless roads, through lanes ankle-deep in mud, to the scattered cottages and home-steads, where perhaps he was turned away with no sale.

Becky went to the barn for rabbit skins which hung, curing, on the warm walls. He turned them over and handed a fine bright sieve, or a strainer, in exchange.

Sometimes he took an order for some coarse lace which he would have next time, or lavender prints for a new dress for Becky, or a sunbonnet. Then he shouldered his pack, lifted the basket on the wall, stooped under it, and hauled it on his head. He walked very stiff and straight down the paths with

good-days fluttering round him, but before he went he solemnly blessed the house and the mistress, for her help.

One day a rival turned up, to try to capture the old man's trade. Margaret shook her head and he became insistent. Then his face lowered and he became threatening. Becky ran to the back door and blew the whistle urgently, one, two, three blasts. They echoed across the fields and Farmer Garland and Dan came out of a fold in the hills. Becky waved a cloth and blew again. They put down their implements and started home at a trot, for the whistle was only used in emergencies or to bring the men to meals.

Margaret went to the dog and began to unloose the excited snarling animal. But the man turned from out of the doorway where he had impudently entered and walked away, cursing and swearing revenge. Becky and Margaret followed him at a distance to see him safely past the buildings down the hill. They returned agitated and fluttering like hens that have been disturbed by a hawk, but triumphant to tell the story to the men whom they saw coming across the near field.

'He won't trouble you again,' said Tom, calming them, and he was right. He returned to the town from which he came. Country folk were too hard-hearted, he said.

Old John Barley, the pig-sticker, came in the autumn to kill the fat pigs for Christmas. He rode over the hills and down the valleys from a far-away village, on a little white pony, long-haired and shaggy, so small that his feet nearly touched the ground on either side. He still wore the country smock-frock, white as milk, embroidered heavily on both shoulders and at the back, but although Joshua wore one, too, for milking – a coarse, heavy, linen frock which Becky found difficult to wash and iron – the pig-sticker wore his all the time. His white beard and whiskers made him look like Rip Van Winkle returning from the Catskill Mountains when he rode down the fields and into the farmyard on his ancient little steed.

But he was not welcome. Susan bade a tearful goodbye to her friends the pigs and retired to the top of the house where she lay with her fingers in her ears, weeping and sick with misery, but often she was away at school when he came.

Dan put the broad wooden bench, the pig-killing table, in the yard, and locked up the dog. Becky boiled the great copper full of water. Joshua sharpened the knives at the grindstone, turning the stone so that it whizzed on the steel.

Then Tom Garland and Dan brought the first happy fat pig, grunting and quietly protesting, from the pig-cote under the lilac trees and elders, now thin and dropping sad leaves, into the paved yard. It trotted, snuffling at the moss, unsuspicious.

When it was seized by Dan and Old Joshua and lifted on the bench it realized its betrayal and resisted with all its might, squealing bitterly. Becky, also protesting, was called out as often as not, to hold a leg, for the pigs were enormous and heavy after their fattening. Tom Garland hated the cries and was very glad when it was over, and the heart-rending human-like shrieks had ceased.

At last the bustle of pork and bacon began. Joints were weighed and sent in baskets covered with clean white cloths to the houses in the villages. Sides were rubbed with salt-petre and carried to stone benches where they lay for weeks. Drip, drip, drip sounded the brine as it dropped in the quiet of night down the runnels and into the brown crocks.

There were scratchings for breakfast, delicious morsels of crisp fat, pork for dinner, trotters for the men's suppers, jellied pork, huge pork pies, big enough for twenty men, besides innumerable brawns and dainties which were sent to the poor in the little villages. But Susan was never happy whilst these sides lay in the back kitchen; she always felt the pigs might come to life again, like Lazarus, and run squeal-ing to ask why they had been slain. Only when they were brought hard and stiff to the kitchen and hung on one of the walls with bunches of thyme and rue, and sage and mar-joram, spreading their perfume over them, did she lose her fear, and know they were no longer pigs, but bacon and hams.

CHAPTER 6

The Circus

'YOU'D better go getting turnips today, Dan,' said Farmer Garland one morning, after Dan had come back from the station with his load of empty churns.

Susan sat wavering over her toast, one eye on Dan and one on the clock. At any moment her father would say, 'It's time for you to be off,' and she would put on her hat and cape, snatch up her bag and run helter-skelter down the garden, past the orchard, and into Dark Wood. She would perhaps dart through the tall buff gate and pick an apple on the way, for the trees were heavy with fruit, and any day now she would find long ladders reared against the trees, and clothes-baskets full of green and red and yellow apples, besides pyramids heaped on the ground in the long thick grass. Yes, a little yellow apple would be best, she thought, from the low knobby tree whose branches she could reach when she jumped. Even as she thought she saw herself leaping with sudden swoops and jumps, her bag flapping at her head, seizing a sweet-smelling apple, half yellow half pink, dangling just within her reach, and snapping off the stiff knotted twig and two leaves.

But Dan's next words sent the apple from her mind, and left it hanging in the tree again.

'There's a circus coming to Broomy Vale this week,' he said, as he stuffed his mouth full of bacon, and waited to see the effect of his announcement.

Susan stared with her cup in the air, her great eyes fixed on his face, as if she would read his inmost thoughts.

'It's a wild beast show, and it's coming for a night,' he mumbled, when he could speak.

'Can I go? Oh! can I go?' Susan jumped up and ran to her father, pulling him by the arm. He took no more notice of her than if she had been a moth.

'Any lions and tigers coming?' he asked slowly, after a long minute spent in meditation, during which Dan's jaws champed, and Susan stood transfixed, longing, listening for a word.

'Aye, there's a power of lions and elephantses, and Tom Ridding says he seen it at Beaver's Den, and it's wonderful what they does.' The words rushed out in a spate, and Dan filled his mouth again and took a noisy drink of tea from his basin.

'Can I go? Can I go?' shouted Susan suddenly, urgently, desperately.

'Be quiet, wench, will ye?' exclaimed Tom, exasperated. He hated to be hurried in his decisions. 'Be off to school with ye.'

'Thank God for a good breakfast,' she said, hastily folding her hands and screwing up her eyes. 'And, please God, let me go to the circus,' she added to herself.

She jumped up on tiptoes to pull down her cape and tam-o'-shanter from the hook behind the door, picked up her satchel and ran off, without thinking of the little yellow apple nodding its head in the misty morning.

She talked of nothing else that day, and all the girls told of the circuses they had seen, clowns and elephants, ponies and lions. Broomy Vale was too far for any of them to go from Dangle, and they begged Susan to remember everything if she went.

'If you're a good girl,' answered her mother, when she got home and asked the question that had danced in her head all day, and that was as much as she could get out of anyone.

On Saturday there was no doubt; they were all going except Becky, who had a hamper of green walnuts to prick, and Joshua, who liked his evenings by the cosy fire.

The milking was over early, and Dan washed his face and polished it with a cloth till it shone like one of the apples.

He changed his corduroys to Sunday trousers, and put on a blue and white collar. He dipped his brush in the lading-can, and sleeked his hair in front of the flower-wreathed little glass. Then, after harnessing the pony in the best pony trap, he left her with a rug on her back, and walked down the hill, with a Glory rose pinned in his cap and a spray of lad's love in his button-hole, to take the field path over the mountain to Broomy Vale.

Mrs Garland wore her purple velvet bonnet trimmed with pansies, which Susan loved and admired so much. She drew a little spotted veil over her face and peeped through like a robin in a cage.

Susan's eyes shone out from under her grey serge hat, which her mother had made and trimmed with the soft feathers from a pheasant's breast. She, too, looked like a bird, an alarmed, excited, joyful hedge-sparrow, as she hopped up and down. On her shoulders she wore the grey cape with a grey fur edge which she wore for school, old-fashioned and homely, lined with scarlet flannel to keep her warm, and this flapped like a pair of wings.

The pony champed her bit and shook her head impatiently with a ring of bells. She softly whinnied and grunted with impatience, and stamped her foot on the stones. Joshua went out and stood by her head, talking soothingly to her.

Becky polished up the trap lamps, and put in fresh candles. Then Tom Garland came downstairs in his Sunday clothes, smelling of lavender, with his horseshoe tie-pin in the spotted silk tie, and a silk handkerchief peeping from his breast pocket. Margaret looked up at him proudly, he was the best-looking man in England, she thought, and Susan put her hand in his.

There was a confused noise of 'Gee-up' and 'Whoa, steady now,' as the pony backed and Margaret and Susan climbed in. Becky stood ready with the rugs and whip, and some chlorodyne lozenges to keep out the night air.

Then Tom Garland followed, bending the shaft with his

weight, as he put his foot on the step. The trap shook and
groaned as he climbed in and gathered up the reins. The
pony ambled slowly down the steep hill, her front feet
slithering as she tried to grip the stones, her haunches high,
the harness creaking. The trap was so tilted that Susan and
Mrs Garland hung on tightly to the back of the seat to keep
from sliding over on Fanny's tail, or suddenly diving on to
her back. Tom Garland's whole attention was spent in holding Fanny up and keeping the trap wheels from catching on
the great stones projecting from the wall on one side, or
running over the bank on the other. The end of the whip
wrapped itself in the blackberry bushes and patches of gorse.
Branches of beech lashed Susan across the face and would
have swept off her hat, but the elastic was tight under her
chin, biting her flesh in a red mark, smelling friendly and
happy, too.

The fog which lay in the valley came up to meet them,
white, writhing, curly shapes, floating along the ground,
climbing the air. Cows in the fields, through which the road
fell, loomed out like giant beasts which hardly stirred until
the trap was almost upon them. At the gates they clustered,
sleepy, rubbing their necks on the smooth warm wood.
Susan jumped out to pull back the latch and hold open each
gate for the pony, and when they had passed she let it go
with an echoing clang as she sprang through the disturbed
cows to the step of the trap.

Fanny always began to run before she got to the bottom of
the hill, as if she rejoiced that the flat easy road was coming.
The trap swayed and rocked as if it would fall over the steep
bank, Tom Garland gripped the reins more tightly, shouting, 'Steady, Fanny, my lass, steady,' and they swung down
to the level turnpike, where the pony tossed her head and
pranced with high steps and jingling bells and hard clicks of
her hoofs, curvetting like a unicorn going to fight a lion.

Broomy Vale was crowded with sightseers. It wasn't often
a circus came to those parts, and everyone with a horse and
cart drove in. Tom went round with the pony to the Bird in

Hand, and Susan and Mrs Garland waited in the street, watching the bands of young men in leggings and bright waistcoats, with flowers in their caps and sticks in their hands escorting young women with gay ribbons round their necks and in their hats, holding up their skirts whether they needed it or not, to show their delicate ankles and fine buttoned boots. There were little families, children shouting and laughing, eyes shining, mouths wide open.

Stout farmers and round-faced shopkeepers, little old ladies in silk mantles, tottering, whiskered old men, greeted them with a 'How d'ye do, Mrs Garland? Fine night for the circus.' For a moment Susan sent a thought winging through the dusky night to the silent hills, to Roger asleep in his kennel, and Becky and Joshua sitting by the fire, pricking the shining green fruit with darning-needles, their stained hands wet with juice. She could smell the rich earthy smell and hear the ticking of the clock, slow and insistent, and the dull roar of the flames. She hugged herself with delight at being in all the bustle and clatter of the little market town.

Children went by, blowing trumpets and twirling noisy wooden clackers, and hanging on to their parents' tails with tightly clenched fists. Babies cried, and were quietened with threats of lions and tigers. Carts rattled down the twisted cobbled street, into the inn yards, lurching against the pavements. Wide-eyed boys leaned against the little shop windows, and clanged the bells as they went in to buy a penn'orth of bulls'-eyes or a stick of liquorice. Above all could be heard the blaring of the brass band outside the circus, and the trumpeting of the elephants.

Tom Garland joined them and they walked along the narrow street, with Susan squeezed between them, towards the circus.

'It fair dithers me to be among all these folk,' said Tom, stopping to look round, and holding up the traffic behind him. 'Where they all come from _I_ don't know. Who'd believe this was Broomy Vale? It's fair thronged, and no mistake.'

'It is,' agreed Margaret. 'I hope we shall get in the wild beast show, that's all. Isn't that Dan over there?'

They saw Dan walking down the middle of the road, wedged in the crowd with a mincing young woman on his arm.

'Hello, that's the cobbler's daughter, as is a dressmaker. I didn't know Dan was walking out with her. He could do better than that, a young woman with a peaky face and no sense. She do look a Jemima in that hat.'

But Dan and his Jemima walked on, unconscious of the criticism.

A vast tent stretched itself in the Primrose Lea, with the river and steep smooth hills on one side, and the churchyard on the other. Around the field were caravans and booths, washing hanging out to dry in the sweet wind, men in blue shirt-sleeves carrying buckets of water. Little foreign babies leaned out from the curtained doors, sucking their fingers, staring with dark eyes at the gaping crowd. Dogs were tethered to the undersides of the blue and red caravans, and here a canary in a brass cage, there a little lamp showed in the cosy interior. These moving homes were as exciting as the wild beasts themselves, which could be heard padding and shuffling in the closed boxes.

But there was no time to look at more. The bandsmen with puffed-out cheeks blew their trombones and beat their drums, and they were swept on to buy their tickets at the gay red and yellow window. They entered the tent with its surprising soft floor of grass, and its moving ceiling of canvas, hanging in lovely folds above their heads, and walked to their places half-way between the red baize-covered seats for the gentry and the low rough forms for the poor people, the ploughboy and the servant girl, the stone-breaker and the hedge-cutter. Susan was so dazzled by the flaring naphtha lights, and so ravished by the savage smells, and so frightened by the roars of wild beasts that she could not see where she was going, and clung blindly to her mother's hand, stumbling over people's feet, kicking their backs. At last they sat down on the high seat, and looked about them at the rows and rows of white faces queerly mask-like under the blazing lamps.

When the clowns came in with painted faces and baggy white trousers and pointed hats, she was too much surprised to laugh. She thought they were rude to the ring-master, and feared they would be sent away for impertinence. Her father laughed loudly at their sallies but she only stared, astonished.

Mrs Garland looked down at her. 'They don't mean it,' she whispered, and Susan smiled faintly as they tumbled about.

But when the animals came in, it was a different matter. Four white horses, with scarlet saddles, and bells hanging from their bridles, danced in sideways. They marched, waltzed, and polkaed round the ring in time to the music of the band. A troupe of tiny Shetland ponies, with tails sweeping the ground, and proud little heads nodding, pranced round, swinging in time, like the veriest fairy horses on a moonlight night. A black mare, glossy as a raven, lay down in the ring, and the riding-master stood on her side to fire a gun. Pigeons flew down from the tent roof, with a ripple of wings, and perched on the gun's barrel, whilst he fired again. They fluttered off, spreading their fan-like tails, and picked up grains of corn from the grass, just like ordinary birds.

'Look at those pigeons! Isn't it a lovely sight?' sighed Margaret happily, and Susan nodded violently. It was so beautiful, she couldn't speak, her eyes and her mind were too busy absorbing all these strange delights.

Then there came a piebald pony with a beautiful girl who only looked about fourteen. She kissed her fingers lightly to the clapping audience, and, with a touch of her fairy foot on the ring-master's hand, she leapt on to the broad back of the pony. Round and round she cantered, all eyes fixed on her young face. The ploughboys cooled towards their lasses and vowed to wed her, if they had to join the circus to do it. Susan decided she would not be a missionary to the heathen

savages. Dan felt in his pocket for the packet of almond rock
he had bought for his young woman; he would give it to this
maid or die.

She stood up with her dainty feet a-tiptoe, dancing up and
down to the motion of the fat little pony with his splashes of
chestnut brown. Her rose-garlanded short skirts with their
frilly petticoats stuck out like a columbine's, and her yellow
curls with the wreath of pink buds floated in the wind behind
her. She must be the happiest person on earth.

The admiring lowly clown held up coloured paper hoops,
and she leapt lightly through, with a soft tear of paper,
alighting safely each time on the wide back beneath. Susan's
hands went up and out in excitement, her fingers trembling,
and Mrs Garland quietly took a hand in hers, and smiled at
her neighbour.

When the young rider finally jumped to the ground, and
kissed and bowed as she led away her pony, Susan clapped
so hard and continued so long after everyone else had
finished, that the people in front stared round to see who
was enjoying it so much.

Dogs came into the ring with frills round their necks and
petticoats round their legs, skipping with the clowns, leaping through barrels. A monkey smoked a pipe and a goat
rang a bell.

There was an outburst from the band and the elephants
entered, the most amazing things of all. Susan had not
imagined they were so immense. She gazed at their large
ears flapping uneasily, their tree-like legs, their curling,
snaky trunks, and compared them with Bonny, the big
draught-horse, who was the largest animal she had seen.
She saw them crashing through the Dark Wood, sweeping
the trees out of their path, trumpeting as they caught her up
and carried her off. They would be welcome, she would run
to meet them. They didn't like the circus, their eyes told her,
and she was sad to see them crouched on little tubs, or
standing in unwieldy fashion on their hind legs. They were
like Samson in the hands of the Philistines, poor giants

captive, waiting for God to tell them to pull down the tent poles and bury the crowd in its folds.

A wave of excitement went over the people when the attendants, in their blue and gold coats, erected the wire cage in the middle of the arena. The smell of the lions, the strange wild-beast scent, affected Susan so that she nearly got up and ran. She watched the muscles ripple in their bodies, and their soundless pad, pad, as they glided across the grass. They looked small and disappointing, she had expected something bigger, grander, but their snarls were so blood-curdling she sat waiting for them to spring among the people. Joshua had told her he once saw a lion bite off a keeper's head, and her father had seen a man's hand mauled. They sat still on their high perches, moving their feet by inches, gazing far away to Africa, whilst the keeper cracked his whip and shot his pistol. How thankful Susan was when it was safely over and they went back to their cages! They were like the shapes and feelings that haunted her in the wood, creeping silently and then springing.

She stood up elated and thrilled to sing 'God save the Queen', which rang through the tent and out into the hills like a paean of praise for deliverance, for many a timid heart had trembled at their first sight of wild beasts.

The drive home in the cold air with lighted lamps under the sparkling sky, so late when she ought to have been asleep, was a fitting climax to the glorious evening. Squeezed between her mother and father, wrapped like a cocoon in rugs, swaying and jolting up and down, as the trap bumped into hollows and rough places, she stared silently up in the sky, whilst Mr and Mrs Garland talked across her of what they had seen.

'It was grand, it was grand,' cried Tom with such conviction that the pony changed her trot to a gallop and had to be calmed down.

'I don't know how they do it, but they say it's all done by kindness,' said Margaret as she clung to the side of the trap.

'Did you enjoy it, Susan?'

A tiny 'Yes' came from the bundle, a faint little whisper. 'She's sleepy, poor child,' murmured her mother, but Susan was wide awake, planning how she could be a circus rider. Fanny seemed her best chance, but Duchess was a nobler-looking mare, with her great hooves which threw up the clods in a shower. It would be fine to stand on her back, among the harness at first for safety, and then with nothing but her mane to cling to. But the farm horses were not so flat, their backs not so table-like as the circus horses, and they were apt to frisk and play. Perhaps Dan would help her; Joshua would have nothing to do with such schemes, she was certain.

They trotted along the hard, ringing roads, past orchards laden with pale globes of green, and rick-yards, mysterious in the dark, through groves of trees which touched hands over their heads, under echoing archways and over the sliding river whose talk drowned the noise of Fanny's hoofs. They passed the toll-gate and more trees, alive, urgent, holding out arms and quivering fingers to the sky, breathing, captive prisoners, under whose star-shadow the travellers dipped. Now and again Fanny saw a ghost, and laid back her ears as she danced sideways, shying at the unknown.

They left behind them the great bulk of a mill, and a row of cottages with lights in the upstair windows. Phantom cats ran across the road, and horses stood with their noses twitching over the gates at the stranger. They passed the lawyer's house, and a high stone archway through which they echoed, and more trees, a turn of the road, a milestone, a cross-road, another village, the gates of Eve's Court, the church, the hill by the river, the ripple of water and their own familiar hillside came in sight.

At the foot of the hill Tom fastened the reins on the splashboard and left the pony to go alone, whilst he and Margaret walked up behind. Up the first steep hill he pushed, and the pony with her head near the ground ran at the difficult slope pulling and straining like the good little lass she was. Her feet sent the stones hurtling down the hill, her muscles stood out. Susan sat, a huddled little figure, nearly tumbling backwards as the trap climbed up under the trees.

Two beams of light streamed on to the hedgerows and banks, illuminating every blade and twig, so that the spiders' webs shone like spun glass, and the leaves were clear as if under a magnifying glass. The rays startled the rabbits and caught the soft eyes of the young cows who had returned to the comfort of the gateways. As they moved up the hill, high trees and low bushes stepped out of the darkness and then disappeared. The lights of Windystone shone down on them from above, like planets in the sky, for Becky had left the shutters unclosed for a beacon.

The pony rested for a few minutes to get her wind and then went on. Again she winded under the oak tree which spread its branches across the path, the recognized 'winding place' for horses from unknown time. Even a new horse slackened and stood still under this tree, without waiting for 'Whoa', as if the mares in the stables had told him the custom. But when a strange servant drove up and urged the horse past the place, he would turn his head with a questioning, protesting look in his patient eyes, as if he were Balaam's ass about to speak.

So Fanny stood there, her sides heaving, as she breathed in deep draughts of the cold fresh air, and again she went on towards the lamplight above.

The Milky Way stretched across the high sky, from the Ridge to the dark beech trees. Auriga rose above the top pasture and hung with flaming Capella on the horizon. The Great Bear swung over the tall stone chimneys which stood out like turrets against the sky, and Vega was there above the branches in the orchard.

The trap rattled into the yard, and pulled up by the front gate. The dog barked, the doors opened, letting out floods of bright light. Joshua appeared with a lantern and took charge of the pony. Susan ran indoors, but Tom Garland stayed a moment to look at the sky. It was good to be there, high up, like an island above the world, near the stars and heaven. His father, his great-grandfather had stood there with the same thoughts on starlight nights, in that kingdom of their own. Then he too turned and walked into the welcoming house, full of firelight and good smells.

Susan lay in bed in her unbleached calico nightgown, imagining herself a golden girl, lightly riding through the air, with flower-bedizened skirts and wreathed head, touching a dappled pony's back ever so lightly with the point of one toe, tossing kisses and roses through the crystal air to a sea of dark people. Round and round went the pony, higher and higher she flew, until through the tent she saw the stars and she fled away among them.

CHAPTER 7

The Secret

SUSAN had a secret which fluttered up and down in her breast, trying to fly out of her mouth. But it mustn't, it must stay down inside or it would be lost for ever. She had whispered it to her bedroom, and now she wanted to tell someone else.

She set the dinner table and ran to the trough for a jug of water. She gave everyone a china mug, and put the teapot on the stove ready for her father's cup of tea. Margaret and Becky hurried in and out of the pantry and larder, carrying cold meat and pickles, bread and cheese and apple pasties. The men came in as they took the roast potatoes from the oven and piled them on the plates. They stamped their feet at the door to knock off the clods and brushed their boots with the yard brush, for not a scrap of earth must come in the kitchen on the red and black tiles. They hung their caps on the hooks, and washed with great splashings and swillings at the sink before they drew their chairs squeaking across the floor and sat down.

Susan sat subdued in the middle, with lowered brows and sulky mouth. 'Children should be seen and not heard' had silenced her. Then she wouldn't tell them, and serve them right. In any case her mother would make her put it in her holly money-box in the hall, or even slip part of it into the box for the Polynesian missions.

She had never had such a large sum in her life before. She pondered ways of spending her secret, whilst the talk flew over her head. Should she buy a mother-of-pearl purse with a spray of flowers painted down one side, and 'A present from Broomy Vale' in curling, flourishing letters down the other? For a year she had longed for this every time she had seen it in Miss Lavender's shop window, when she had gone with her father to the big market. Whilst he looked at the cows and poked their sides, or rubbed the backs of the sheep in the pens, or went for a word with Joshua who had charge of the calves sent from Windystone, she sat patiently in the cart holding the reins, and eating a bun from a paper bag. She could see the purse, amid tea-cosies and egg-timers, crochet mats and shell boxes.

Or should she get a brooch with her initial on it, S for Susan? A silver one, perhaps with her whole name. A safety ink bottle was most desirable, made of red leather, or a book. *A Thousand and One Arabian Nights' Entertainment* floated in her mind. Where had she heard of it? 'Arabia, Arabia,' she murmured softly, and she caught the clock's eye and nodded. She peered behind at the settle. They knew she had something to tell them when she was alone with them. 'Arabia, Arabia.'

'Don't chunter, Susan, and get on with your dinner,' scolded Margaret.

In the afternoon when Becky had gone upstairs to change her dress, and her father with Dan and Joshua were in the fields breaking in the foal, an experiment she loved to watch, she came back to the house and stood in the passage, soft-stepping, mysterious. She turned the handle and waited outside the door a moment before entering just to give everything a chance to get back to its place again. Then she stepped lightly in. There was no one, but the air vibrated and trembled with words which had just flown across. For a moment the room was surprised at being caught, and then it welcomed her. She rubbed her finger slowly and medita-tively along the oak dresser, rough under its polish with ridges of wear, pitted with shot where a gun had accidentally gone off a hundred years ago, but as fresh in the memory as yesterday. The tall-boy sent out warm delicious homely smells of cinnamon, camomile, ginger and tea; the grand-father clock ticked loudly, and then changed his voice to a

softer note, as she listened with quick-beating heart and intense love. They all understood her, even before she spoke, they wanted to tell her they were glad of her, that however far away she went, even if she grew up, they would remain the same, her faithful friends.

She had lain alone for hours, a tiny girl, fastened in the settle by a board which hooked across the front, making a house for her. She had listened to the clock with its varying tick, and the crackling fire, she had watched the flies circling round the ceiling, content and amused by the little sounds which flickered round the room, aware of a presence which protected her whilst her mother and father were out driving to the big town, or visiting the farms and markets eight or ten miles away, leaving the men working in the fields, and the girl busy with all her odd jobs. When they returned they marvelled at her patience, and never knew she had so many friends.

She opened her mouth to speak, her voice took on a soft, low, musical tone as she half whispered, 'I've got a secret. Shall I tell you? Do you want to know?'

She felt a stir but nothing moved, all was expectant, as she gazed lovingly at each piece of furniture, letting her eyes move deliberately round the room, her thoughts dwelling on each, so intimately near, closer than her parents or school friends.

'I have won a half-crown piece,' she announced with triumph. The clock shook and whirred as he drew himself up and solemnly struck three. Susan waited till the echoing chime had died away and then continued. 'I won it for recitation, from the vicar of Dangle. A new half-crown,' and she dived in her pocket and brought it out shining white.

'And shall I tell you what I'm going to do? I shall buy a book with it, called' – and here she paused to impress the room – '*A Thousand and One Nights*.' She waited again, and the room was all ears.

'A thousand and one tales, it will last me nearly three years, and sometimes I will read bits of it to you. It's about a far country, Arabia.'

'Arabia,' murmured the room sleepily.

'Arabia,' cried the fire and the words floated up the chimney out into the sky.

'I recited "The Spacious Firmament", and I will say it to you. Listen,' and she stood on the rag hearth-rug with her back to the fire and faced the room and its listeners. She lifted her head to the bright gun slung across the ceiling, and in a low, quiet, vibrating voice recited Addison's hymn:

> *The spacious firmament on high*
> *With all the blue ethereal sky,*
> *And spangled heavens, a shining frame,*
> *Their great Original proclaim.*
> *Th' unwearied sun from day to day*
> *Does his Creator's power display;*
> *And publishes to every land*
> *The work of an Almighty hand.*
>
> *Soon as the evening shades prevail,*
> *The Moon takes up the wondrous tale;*
> *And nightly to the listening Earth*
> *Repeats the story of her birth:*
> *Whilst all the stars that round her burn,*
> *And all the planets in their turn,*
> *Confirm the tidings as they roll,*
> *And spread the truth from pole to pole.*
>
> *What though in solemn silence all*
> *Move round the dark terrestrial ball;*
> *What though nor real voice nor sound*
> *Amidst their radiant orbs be found?*

In Reason's ear they all rejoice,
And utter forth a glorious voice;
For ever singing as they shine
'The Hand that made us is divine'.

At the end she bowed and waited for a moment with her fingers tightly clasped, and a rapt expression on her face.

'That's all.'

A force electrified the room, and the air trembled with thoughts and waves of feeling from the things unseen. Then away she went to the Whitewell field to watch the paces of the foal, and forgot the waiting listeners in her pleasure.

She hid her half-crown under her mattress, but Becky discovered it and had to be pledged to secrecy. She hid it again in a hole under a tree, and there it lay for a week. Then she begged to go to Broomy Vale with her father. But whilst he sat in the barber's shop, she fastened the reins round the handle of the brake and went boldly to the bookshop.

Yes, they had it in a cheap edition, small print and poor paper, bound in red cloth. She carried it back and hid it under her cape. It was disappointing on the outside, and there were no pictures, but there was a tremendous lot of reading. She pored over it in bed when she should have been asleep, sitting up with her candlestick on the pillow. But her mother looked up from the water-trough and saw the little light dancing through the window. She hurried upstairs and the stairs cried out to warn Susan, who popped her book down among the bedclothes, blew out the candle and shut her eyes.

She was betrayed by a little grey curl of smoke which hovered in the air over her face, an accusing finger pointing down at her. Mrs Garland took away the *Thousand and One Nights* for ever.

It nearly put out the kitchen fire, but the damper was drawn out, and it flamed away, up the chimney, through the boughs of the whispering elm, to the wood, where it sank in black flakes among the beech and chestnut trees, dropping to the earth with their fluttering gold leaves.

Susan found another book, with stories nearly as exciting as those in the ill-fated Arabian Nights. There was no love in this book, only terrors, no Peri, only Death, no Paradise, only a raging, burning hell.

It was a thick, solid little book called *The Tower of Faith*, full of short stories which the child read greedily. She was terrified by it, but she could not keep away.

Death hid on every page ready to fall on the wicked, to punish the thoughtless, to confound the ungodly. The children in the book all did exactly as Susan would have done, she felt here was a mirror of herself, warning her in time of her probable, no, certain fate. There was no escape from the all-seeing eye.

There was the story of the boy who went bird-nesting when he should have been at church. He was caught in a storm and killed by lightning, and his poor burnt bones were found lying in the fields by his parents.

There was a saucy miss who turned up her nose at good meat, and came to beg at the houses of her school friends, a thin scarecrow of a woman, desolate and ragged.

There was the girl who wrote her own epitaph in a moment of merriment and died at the very date she had given. Susan was so thrilled by this that she sat down at once with paper and pencil to write hers. She put it in a drawer and kept the date in memory, but as the time approached she got so alarmed she tore it up, and the day passed safely by.

There was, too, the careless non-religious girl who heard a warning voice. She said, 'God bless you' to her mother as she left for her work in the morning, but when she returned her mother was dead. She was so thankful her last words had been good that she turned then and there to religion.

The stories of warning voices made a deep impression on Susan. She had always felt life to be insecure. At nine years old death might come at any moment. The religion of the time fostered these feelings, the texts decorating the walls were a preparation for death. Any time, too, the world might come to an end, and flare up like a piece of tissue paper, or tinder from a rotten tree.

Children at school said that anyone who told a lie might be struck dead like Ananias; one child even knew someone who died that way. You might die in your sleep, too, and Susan was quite glad to awake alive.

Each morning she prepared for the worst. She left the house for school feeling she might never see her parents again; little conscience voices continually warned her. She kissed them 'Goodbye' with such deep affection they were quite touched by her devotion, and she cried 'God bless you' so fervently, like a pastor blessing his congregation, running back up the hill to say it if she forgot, that Mrs Garland felt her prayers had not been in vain.

Every evening she was thankful to see them again, to find the house not destroyed by earthquake or fire, the dog still in his kennel, the cows in the fields. Equally thankful, too, she was that she had not been spirited away in the wood on the way home.

Life was uncertain, strange and unreal, but she had so many secret friends she could not be sad. In the house the clock and dresser shared many of her joys. The high-backed chair in the corner with the carved face in the back and the blue and white check cushions was glad when she sat on it. The four-legged stool on which generations of servant boys had perched, its seat worn by many corduroy trousers, the big oak cupboard, the Chinese jugs, and the teapot with an old woman on the top, even the hole in the floor recognized her and spoke.

But the clock was the most human of all, the clock which had never been moved except for the annual cleaning since her great-grandfather had dragged himself up on petti-coated knees and peeped through the little bull's-eye window, with the brass frame, at the shining pendulum wagging to and fro. Susan had known it to stop and listen, too, when she sat alert for the sound of a wolf snuffling at the door on a winter's night. Sometimes it sighed so audibly that Susan's heart ached, and it grunted and wheezed like an old man when the weather was stormy and rheumatism was about.

When Susan's grandfather had died it stopped, and would not go again until after the funeral. It knew a lot, it had stood there when cattle plague raged on the farm and destroyed every animal, when tragedy visited the house, when fever and death took away the old and the young, whom only it remembered. It was alive, that clock, and Susan's friend.

CHAPTER 8

Trees

TREES had always had a strange fascination for Susan, ever since she had lain, an infant wrapped up in a shawl, in a clothes-basket in the orchard, babbling to the apple trees and listening to their talk. They are queer, half-human creatures, alive yet tied to the ground. Lucky they are tied, too, for rooted they are safe.

One night Susan dreamed she looked through the big window in the kitchen, past the bright milk cans reared upon the wall, to the stretch of fields rolling up to the crest of hills in the north. She saw a company of mighty trees, beeches, oaks, and elms of prodigious size, walk over the sky-line, sweeping down the hills to the fields, a giant assemblage of shining ones with branches waving like a hundred arms, vast trunks moving serenely but terribly, and green hair of leaves shaking in the wind.

The cows and horses started up affrighted, her father and mother paled in horror, as they stared with her through the window, and she stood transfixed, aghast, listening to the approaching rustle like the sound of the sea, waiting for these gods to destroy the house and farm, as they walked through them to the hills of the sky in the south.

She awoke in great fear, and told her dream the next day. Margaret called it nonsense, a nightmare, but Tom looked serious, he knew the trees, and had heard a cry when the woodmen cut down the great oak where the plantation now stood, a cry of anguish.

But the ash, Susan's friend, was none of these. It stood free-growing, graceful, with branches tossing like the arms of a dancer, when the south wind blew across the plough field and orchard bringing the scent of flowers and carrying bees from the skeps under the apple trees.

Cows sheltered under its wide-stretching boughs when the rain beat down the long leaves and the wind came bellowing like a maddened bull up the field from the deep valley and the great hills beyond, lashing its branches and tearing them, so that they lay, with black knotted fingers on the ground. It was sheltered from the east wind and the north by the hills that circled close to it, but the west wind tried to sweep it away.

In the hottest summer days, when haymaking was over, red and dappled cows, and white-faced Herefords, stood by its great trunk, frisking their tails, gently shaking their heads, waiting to be called to the milking-sheds.

In the winter it stood stark and bare like a naked witch. Then its long arms beckoned and waved, beseeching, imploring, menacing. Susan came to it and talked, she tried to pacify it, laying her cheek against its wet trunk, and her hands on its bark.

But when snow fell it was a white lady, a queen, mysterious, silent, desiring nothing, possessing all.

One summer day Susan lay under its branches, listening to the multitude of sounds around her. At the edge of the field, in the wood, the fir trees moaned like waves on the sea-shore, as if they had a little wind of their own chained to their boughs, but under the ash the wind sang softly. The sycamores quivered their silver-lined leaves, nodding to those who could understand. Flies droned and bees hummed, and little green frog-hoppers bobbed on her hands with the tiniest thuds of their geometrical bodies. The pulse of the wind dropped so low every few seconds that she heard the faint flutter of flower petals dropping near her on the grass. By the side of the bridle-path the gorse pods popped like fairy cannons shooting the grasshoppers.

Against the background of the wind's sound was the music of bird-song, chirps and twitters, quavers and ripples. One little bird ran down the scale, and another sang a tiny

monotonous dirge of two notes, ting-tong, like water dropping from a well.

Another sound, very faint but familiar, began to pene-
trate her consciousness. She put her ear to the ground to
listen, and the tinkle was more distinct. Near by was a flat
stone which she had seen before, half hidden in the long
grass, sunken in the earth so that the mowers' scythes were
unharmed when they went over it. She raised one corner
with great difficulty, using all her young strength, and the
sound rose like imprisoned music escaping from a hidden
orchestra. She tugged again and dragged the stone aside.
Underneath was a hole, wet, sweet-smelling of earth. Deep
down a tiny jet of water played like a fountain, whispering,
purling, rising and falling, curved and flowing like a mare's
tail of glass, down in the dark ground. She covered it
again with the stone, the secret the ash tree had always
known.

In the same field close to the path was an oak, a rough
giant, with boughs as thick as any ordinary tree trunk. Its
great girth was surrounded by a seat on which generations
had sat to love, to plan, to weep. Smock-frocks and crinolines, old bonneted women, tired old men, babies and careless children had leaned back against the bole, with its
medley of knots and humps. It was full of ghosts.

Three times it had been struck by lightning, but the tree
remained a splendid creature, dignified by the name 'The
Oak', as if it were the only one, instead of one in hundreds.
It was Susan's nursery. In cavities in its sides she kept her
toys, and from the shoots springing from the round bosses she
hung her pipe of elder, and her triangle. In the hollows between its roots she made a kitchen with acorn food and a
bed of leaves.

A swing hung from one great horizontal bough, and here
she spent many hours. In the dusk she came, when the snow
was thick on the ground, and the air cut like knives, and in
midsummer she lolled there with a book. The tree was on
the edge of a sudden dip, a steep fall into a valley. Susan felt

like a bird swooping across the fields, only to be pulled back
to the tree again.

But twice the tree had tried to kill her. The long iron
chains jerked treacherously one day
and threw her off. She fell with her
head on a piece of rock jutting
through the thin bare soil. She was
carried home, bathed in blood, by
her troubled father and stitched up
by the village doctor.

For a time she kept away from
the tree, and then she played again
beneath it. Weeks later she sat
swinging slowly, looking across the
valley to the little white roads
which climbed the hills and disappeared over the top. She had
never been over them, they led to
wild country, where there were no
trees, and no rivers, only moorland
and waste places.

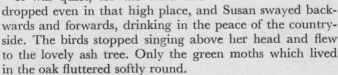

It was quiet, for the wind had
dropped even in that high place, and Susan swayed backwards and forwards, drinking in the peace of the country-
side. The birds stopped singing above her head and flew
to the lovely ash tree. Only the green moths which lived
in the oak fluttered softly round.

Then Susan heard a tiny sound, so small that only ears
tuned to the minute ripple of grass and leaf could hear it. It
was like the tearing of a piece of the most delicate fairy
calico, far away, hidden, deep, as if an elf were making new
sheets.

She took no notice, but an absurd unreasoning terror
seized her. The Things from the wood were free. She sat
swinging, softly swinging, but listening, holding her breath,
always pretending she did not care.

Her heart's beating was much louder than the midget rip,

rip, rip, which wickedly came from nowhere. She looked up at the tree, but there was nothing, no motion, not even a bird who might have made the sound deep in his tiny throat, as he whispered to himself a tune.

A voice throbbed in her head, 'Go away, go away, go away,' but still she sat on the seat, afraid of being afraid.

Then aloud, to show Them she was not frightened, she sighed and said, 'I am so tired of swinging, I think I will go,' and she slid trembling off the seat and walked swiftly away, the blood drumming in her ears, drowning the exquisitely small sound.

Immediately the rip grew to a thunder like a giant hand tearing a sheet in the sky, and the whole enormous bough fell with a crash which sent echoes round the hills. The oaken seat of the swing was broken to fragments, the rock was split, and the great chains bent and crushed.

Susan stood frozen, bewildered, just outside the reach of the tree. The bough lay like a full-grown oak, torn off, fresh, quivering, the oak tree stood inimical, hating, and Susan never moved.

From the farm Tom Garland rushed out, followed by the men and Becky. The dog barked, and the horse and mares galloped across the fields.

'Susan, Susan,' shouted Tom from the gate. 'Susan,' he cried, trembling with fear as he came to her, 'I thought you'd been crushed to death. What happened? How did you escape? I heard the oak drop its bough with a noise of a house falling, and I hardly durst look; I knew you were swinging.'

Susan never answered as she was led away.

'It was God that took care of her,' said Mrs Garland. 'He warned her,' and she took the child in her arms on the rocking-chair and rocked to and fro.

Susan kept silent, she could not speak of Them, they might hear, but old Joshua said, 'Trees are like that, they drop without warning when they want to kill.'

The other oaks were friendly; Susan climbed their

branches and played among their boughs. The beeches, too, with their low-dipping whispering branches loved her. There were two in particular which grew by the side of a cow path, with fox-gloves round their feet. Their trunks were so large that three men could not span them, and their great roots ran along the earth in twists and knots, forming tables and seats, cupboards and caves.

They were the survivors of a wood that had been cut down when Susan was born and planted with oaks and firs, a sinister plantation where foxes and weasels lived. But the 'beechen trees' were of different mould, too noble to stoop to scare a child. The first cuckoo perched on the wishing-gate underneath their branches in the spring and called to the echo, 'Cuckoo, Cuckoo'. Rabbits ran through the wandering roots and made their burrows, red squirrels danced along the high grey boughs, and flashing magpies flirted their tails. Susan sat underneath with her mug of warm milk straight from the cow, with minute gnats imprisoned in the froth, and Becky brought her knitting in the summer. Away in the far pasture was a group of limes which attracted Susan first by the music of their bee-filled branches, and then by the scent of their honey flowers. They were the only limes for miles round, and their discovery was a great event. Three trees sprang from one root, and by stepping on a pile of stones Susan could climb into the green bower and sit lost in a world of leaves.

But the spot was too lonely except for a casual visit. It was more than a mile away, in the last field, on the border of a wilderness of precipitous wood with trees scrambling among masses of rock, dwarf and misshapen trees, long leafless hags of trees, lightning-blasted and ivy-slain trees, with old mine-workings under their roots, the pits covered with loose stones and carpeted with nettles and forget-me-nots. A deserted broken-down cottage lay in ruins, with broken walls leering among the bushes, and badgers, foxes, and rats made their homes under the ground.

Cries of rabbits made her catch her breath, quiet rustlings

of adders startled her as she looked down from her eyrie in the trees.

Sometimes she glimpsed the welcome figure of a poacher, scrambling over the rocky ground, trampling the ferns and sending the blackbirds screaming with rage past the quiet figure in the lime trees, to the sunny fields beyond. So Susan visited these outposts only when she wandered with Becky or her mother, picking mushrooms and blackberries, or when the haymakers were in the neighbouring fields, and the chatter and laughter of the Irishmen drove away all ghosts, but she waved to them, across the intervening fields, beautiful ladies in a hostile country.

In winter she felt as close to her trees as in the summer, and she struggled through snowdrifts to visit them, as they stood white under the freezing sky, waiting for the word. In summer she laid gifts of flowers at their roots, or slipped a posy in their bark, a little offering in return for their friendship, a touch of colour on the dark trunks.

From the grove of silver birch trees, on the edge of Druid Wood, the birch rod, which hung in a corner of the kitchen among the lanterns and stirrups, was cut, and bound with withies. It had a hundred stings, and Susan had tasted it too often to look at the trees with equanimity. She was brought up under the shadow of the proverbs, 'Spare the rod and spoil the child', 'Early to bed, early to rise, makes a man healthy, wealthy, and wise', 'Wilful waste makes woeful want', and they ruled her life.

'You'll come to want,' warned Mrs Garland, when Susan turned up her nose and refused to eat her meat and rice pudding, two things she detested. 'There's many a one who is beggar now, going from door to door, through leaving her good food.'

This gave her a fright. Beggars sometimes came to the old Hall, pitiful creatures with broken shoes and ragged dresses. Mrs Garland gave them bowls of hot broth and made them sit down on the steps by the rose trees to drink it whilst she found some more shoes and an old dress or hat for them to carry away. It was so far from the village and the hill such a climb, they deserved everything they got, she said. But Susan trembled to think she might become one of these poor things, and she gulped down her food.

Then one day when she was returning home from school running down the road with some other girls, in a spirit of bravado she threw a bad-smelling crust into the muddy road.

'I don't want that silly old crust,' she boasted, and they all laughed.

She left the children at the village and climbed up the fields to Dark Wood, but no sooner had she entered than the thought of the crust began to trouble her. The trees surrounded her, whispering more than usual, heavy and sinister. Her steps lagged, a pain grew in her breast, a queer miserable pain. If she left that crust she would as surely come to want as night follows day. She couldn't bear it any longer. She turned round, tired as she was after a long day, and went back. Two miles away she found it lying in the dirt where she had thrown it. She picked it up and rubbed it in her handkerchief, and returned it to her bag. Her heart was light, the wood seemed brighter, although it was quite dark before she got home.

She gave a thankful sigh of escape from certain unhappiness as she crept slowly through the gate and threw the crust to Roger. He gobbled it up and asked for more, but she had learnt her lesson.

On Sunday nights Margaret had family prayers to which everyone came. They knelt on the hard floor, with their faces buried in their hands, in a semi-circle with their backs to the fire, Becky, Dan and Joshua, Mr and Mrs Garland and Susan. It was a time Susan loved, she felt that God was in the kitchen, a kind spirit, hovering like a flame above their heads, listening to the prayers in the quiet room. The clock ticked softly, listening too, the fire gently sighed and crackled in the grate, and the wind moaned outside the door like evil shut out.

Each listened as Mrs Garland read the words from the Prayer Book, the prayer for fine weather or rain, the prayer for the sick, the General Thanksgiving and the Lord's Prayer. Each one felt safe in the hands of Heaven. Hell was forgotten, God was a father, and His advice was asked over all difficulties.

The room was full of holy thoughts. A dove folded its wings across the ceiling, and peace surrounded them.

CHAPTER 9

Lantern Light

THE morning air was sweet with autumn scents, falling elm leaves, bent ferns, bruised wet grass, beech leaves and syca-more. Windfalls, from the great tree that was too old and too tall to climb, dropped with little thuds and lay under Fanny's feet, crunching under her hoofs as she fed on the patch of grass by the gravelled drive.

Everywhere there was a sound of dropping, tiny bumps filled the air, some so soft that only the blackbird heard, the fall of the scarlet fruit from the dark yews, the beech mast littering the woods. The sweet chestnuts bounded on the paths, splitting open and exposing their one sweet kernel and two withered ones. Dan picked them up and ate them, and kicked away the husks. Susan hunted among the leaves and feasted.

Late Glory roses, tea roses with peach-coloured hearts and petals shading to the deepest cream, bloomed on the house, faded, and scattered their brown leaves on the grass beneath. A few chrysanthemums were left, tawny red flowers and little maroon buttons on the green dresses of the bushes.

Sprigs of lad's love lay among the clothes in the oak presses, and the children at school wore bunches of it to keep them healthy now the damp mists were about.

The woods all round the house were heavy with rich-smelling fallen leaves and decaying moss, with scarlet toad-stools and enormous fungi which, when Susan kicked them, turned deep purple, the sure sign they were the deadliest of dead poisons, the food of witches.

The robin's note had changed. He twisted the corkscrew in infinitesimal bottles and poured out the sparkling, chuckling winedrops. He became bolder, the little visitor who was always welcome, and stepped with light foot and engaging eye into the shadow of the doorway to see what there was for breakfast. No cats lived at Windystone Hall, to drink the milk and kill the chicks and scare the robins, so he had no one to fear.

Pheasant strolled proudly across the meadows, and carelessly pecked the turnips which lay in the plough fields.

They knew they were safe so long as they did not go in the gardens or orchard. Twenty rabbits sat in a hollow of the field, under the crooked crab-apple tree, which leaned its branches down weighted with green crabs. Susan clapped her hands as she stood at the door, to make their white tails bob, but they, too, didn't care.

Dan came in with a capful of mushrooms, silvery globes and buttons from the Daisy Spot. Tom climbed the filbert trees and filled the big round basket to the brim with the frilled and petticoated nuts.

Pears were ripe round the south parlour window, and their pointed leaves tried in vain to hide them.

The autumn days went slowly by, dragging the last warm apricots and crimsons from the sun. It was a time of mother-of-pearl mists, changing to soft reds and yellows as the sun gained its puny strength, and then lengthened into shadows.

The gables of Windystone were pricked out on the steep fields, like a colony of tall houses inhabited by a race of giants. Phantom black smoke rose from the shadow chimneys, and ran up the hill. The haystacks, too, spread out their gabled shadows, and pretended to be black witches' cottages with living, breathing old women waiting for dark to ride up into the sky on the broomsticks which lay against the barns. Grotesque, dusky cows, with lanky legs sprawling up the trees and banks, cropped beside the sleek velvet-eyed creatures with their red satiny coats and white faces.

Flocks of little clouds ran over the sky, driven hither and thither by the dogs of the wind, until they too, like the shadows, went over the mysterious rim of the world.

The world's end was very near Windystone, just up a field and a steep scramble through Druid's Wood, with its dense trees and bracken, its crumbly, leafy soil which broke under the foot, and the horizon was reached. A stark naked, blasted tree stood with white bleached boughs on the edge against the sky, as if to proclaim the fact that there was nothing more.

When Susan was little she had thought that if ever she got up here the world would fall right away, down, down, for ever. But when she was taken to the top she found a soft green field, dropping slowly to beech wood and valleys beyond. So the edge of the world was pushed further away, but even when she was nine and very wise she would not have been surprised to find the ultimate precipice beyond one of those hills.

Mornings began with mists like pools of milk upset in the valleys, into which Susan ran helter-skelter to school. Gossamer, beaded with jewels, bound together the bracken and heather, the trees and ferns. The briars, the hedgerows, the bushes were covered with millions of tiny webs, beaded like fair necklaces with dewdrops. Her feet broke silvery meshes spread like a net over the wet grass, and she left dark footprints as if she walked in snow. Soon the first hoar-frost would come, powdering the world, making a wood a vast jeweller's shop in the morning, a haunted palace at night.

Down the lane the briar hung in circles and garlands with

ruddy-veined leaves and cursed ill-luck late blackberries. Susan picked up fallen acorns and gathered bunches of nuts as she skipped through the wood, families of five and six on a stem, which she took to school.

She snatched branches of hawthorn and ate the fleshy crimson aiges as her breakfast dessert, washing them down with water from a spring which ran through the bracken.

The hawthorns and hollies were full of field-fares and red-wings, clearing away the fruit like ragamuffins let loose in a greengrocer's shop. Squirrels ran up and down the nut trees and beeches, carrying nuts to their hoards.

At the farm the work in the plough fields was at its height. Abel, the ditcher, and Noah Smith came to help gather the potatoes and store them in trenches with a few for the house in the old cow place. Mangolds were pulled and beheaded, and piled in great mounds like the barrows of the Stone men who had lived there once. Hedges were trimmed and the cuttings fired in numerous little bonfires.

Bonfire day passed with the great roaring fire in the corner of the plough field, when potatoes were roasted under the stars and tiny Chinese crackers flew through the air.

Susan had never heard of Guy Fawkes, nor had Tom or Becky, or Joshua. It was a 'Bun Fire', when they ate parkin and treacle toffee, and children danced round the fire before winter swept the fields.

As it died they leapt through the low flames and each had a wish. Then they stood in the fields to watch the other fires, on the hills in the distance, before they went in to their early bed.

Nights were nearly dark when Susan came home through the wood. Shadows were about and things peeped at her. Then one night the wind bumped into her like a butting lamb ready for play. The beech trees rose and fell with dull roars, and thick grey clouds ran across the sky, with arms intertwined, closer and closer, until, like a mob of children, they raced into school beyond the outermost hill.

But the wind became stronger and bellowed like a bull,

and fiercer, blacker clouds covered the sky. The trees rocked in excitement as if they knew what was coming and rejoiced in the battle. They were free, they moved, the boughs creaked and rattled their bones. Winter was coming, galloping up with the cold blasts from the North Pole, and the world shook.

Susan struggled up the hill to the orchard; the straw lying loose in the stack-yard rose and danced on its ends; the loose boards over the grain-pit flapped up and down like the slippers of an untidy woman. Hens were blown, crying and cackling, with feathers awry, as they fled to the hen-house, and scrambled up the narrow little stairway which ran along the side of the wall.

The wind seized Susan's skirts and blew them over her head. She was intensely vexed and embarrassed, although there was no one to see but the weathercock-man, who twirled madly on top of the stable. She dragged them down with one hand while she clutched her hat with the other, and fought her way to the door, breathless against the buffeting wind.

Dan, Joshua, and Becky were struggling across the grass from the big cow-house with full pails of milk which the wind splashed on their clothes. Everybody walked with head bent forward to get through the gale.

The cows were kept indoors for the winter, only the young stirks with their rough coats and the calves and sheep stayed out, and they had open shelters to which they could retreat.

The men came into the house bringing packets of cold sweet air entangled in the rough wool of their coats, the smell of cows in their hair, and the good scent of earth on their boots. Their checks and eyes shone, their skin was clear and rosy.

Margaret laughed as she trimmed and lighted the lamp and hung it over the table. Becky and Susan went round the house, cottering the kitchen and dairy shutters which closed on the outside, latching the great oak shutters of the parlours, hall, and stone room, which were folded in the thickness of the walls.

Tom reached down the horn lantern with its pointed top like a roof and the little hole in the side where the draughts blew the flame awry, and Dan fetched the new hurricane lamp, with shiny glass and bright cage. They measured and 'scyed' the milk.

Dan drove down to the station with the night's supply, and the rest sat round the table eating great puffy roast apples bathed in cream, crisp celery with deep sweet hearts, and plates heaped with crusty home-made bread and butter.

The wind howled round the house like a wolf, whining under the doors, screaming down the wide chimneys. The flames were driven out into the room and then roared up the chimney. Margaret brought out the new sacking and the pieces of cloth she had collected during the year, good parts of worn-out trousers, coats, and skirts. She and Becky cut them into strips and started to peg the rug which was their winter work.

Joshua sat by the fire with the *Farmer and Stockbreeder*. Tom reached down a little black lantern from a corner cupboard and polished it with a soft cloth. Then he hung it from a hook on the ceiling. The next day Susan, too, must have a light to bring her home from school.

In the night the wind dropped and went into his den to sleep ready for another attack on the trees. But the leaves had gone, all but a few odd ones which Susan watched from day to day, waiting to see how long they could stay. The country looked naked, and bare, the trees were stripped for the fight. Only the fir trees waved their dark boughs up and down, with the regularity of a clock, sighing happily.

Margaret wrapped a scarf round Susan's neck, and gave her a box of matches and the lantern when she sent her off to school. Susan felt proud and grown-up, elated as an explorer.

She hid the lantern under a stone by the gate at the end of the wood ready for night.

She asked the teacher to let her out at four o'clock without waiting for the pin to drop, or late prayers.

When she returned to the wood, dusk had already fallen. She opened the little door of the lantern and held it under her cape. Then she struck a match, sheltering it with her curved body, and lit the bit of candle. She quickly closed and latched the door, and the brave little light shone out, clear through the clean glass she had polished with her handkerchief, breathing and rubbing as she had seen old Joshua polish the trap lamps.

Ruby red came through the side windows, but they were so small and the candle so wee they only made a glow. Even the smell of the japanned metal was comforting, and the tiny curl of smoke warmed her fingers as it came through the top, under the handle.

The difference the light made was surprising. It might have been a holy candle and Susan a little saint walking unharmed and unafraid through the terrors of hell.

She felt valiant and brave as she walked in the dark shadows, with trees hemming her in and the candle throwing a gleam like a fire-fly among the branches and on the black path.

She felt invisible, like the prince in the fairy tale, wrapped in a cloak of darkness, fenced round by security, with the light dancing along ahead in slender beams of gold.

She flashed the lantern on the hideous wall, herself safely hidden behind it, and the evil eyes turned away. She held it towards the menacing oak tree, and the Things shrank back as before a magic sword.

Sometimes the wind slashed the trees so that they shrieked and rocked together with boughs interlaced, a wild mad wood, and the candle wavered and trembled ready to go out. Then she carried it under her cloak, where it was a secret joy, a little hidden fire, at which she peeped as she walked stumbling in the darkness.

But if the wind really conquered and extinguished her lantern, she never stopped to light it again, but trudged on, battling with her head forward, pressed against the wind, defenceless, lost, ready for death at any moment, until she reached the safety of the fields beyond.

So she climbed up the hills to the light beckoning her at the top, where the farm, like Noah's Ark, with all its animals safe inside, floated in the sea of darkness, cut off from the drowned black world outside.

CHAPTER 10

Moonlight

THE sky was like an apple tree hung with myriads of little gilt apples as Susan looked up at it from the lonely stillness of the wood-field, where the stirks stood half asleep under the hawthorn trees, knee-deep in red bracken. Her father had told her there would be a moon tonight so she would not need the lantern.

She waited, staring up to the stars, and watching a soft light steal from behind a great peaked hill like a sugar cone, across the river. She was first at the meeting-place, the moon was late.

Then he came round the corner of Stark Hill, just in time to light her through the wood, which lay like a black cave in front of her. The gate shone bright and the stone posts glimmered.

Susan walked along with her eyes on the moon's golden face. The path was dim, but she was unafraid, for the crowding trees were asleep, the powers were harmless, and the moon, this spiritual unearthly friend, was her companion.

At school she had a reputation for bravery which she didn't deserve. The teachers stared at her as she set off, dressed in her little grey cloak and wool mittens, on her four-mile walk in the gathering dark, which would swallow her up when the other children were all sitting round their fires at home or playing by their cottage doors. They never suspected her heavenly friend waiting up in the blue.

She stared up at the moon and his dark eyes stared back at her as he swam along the sky by her side. One night she had turned her eyes away, the path was uneven and rough and she had stumbled against the bank and fallen into a pit of brown leaves. So she looked down on the ground. But when she turned to the moon again, he had stopped behind! Hot and alarmed she ran back, and fixing her eyes on his face, she started off again, with the moon alongside.

He floated through the boughs of the trees, thin now the leaves had gone, and made her path silver, mottled and fretted with dancing shadows. The pools in the few level places shone out and she walked round them dry-shod.

When she got to the end of the wood he stood still above the lovely valley, with the twisty river like a silver snake, writhing at the bottom, and the broad white road alongside like a second river, and the square fields with black walls, a chess-board on the slopes of the hill, and another tiny chess-board higher up, and a glittering one all soft and lost under the moon himself. Round the edge was a fringe of black wood, going up to the sky, and when she climbed up to Windystone the fringe would go right round the cup of the world.

She left him there, and walked gaily on, swinging her dinner-bag, whistling merrily, in spite of her father's adage, 'Whistling women and crowing hens deserve to have their heads chopped off', for she was looking for shooting stars. Every night in the winter she saw one, sometimes many, and for every star she had a wish.

Now she was clear of the wood she could see her moon shadow, running along the wall by her side.

'A moon shadow must never be trodden upon,' said Joshua, and she looked curiously at the frail thing which fluttered from her feet. There were so many kinds of shadows, all different in their feelings, sun and moon, solid and ghostly, lamplight and candlelight, homely and goblin.

She turned back at the top of the steep steps to rest a minute and recover her breath. She looked across the tops of the apple trees to where the moon stood waiting with soft clouds and rainbow veils across his face. He threw them off with a smiling gesture, and shone with all his might.

'Good night, Moon; thank you,' she called, and her voice floated across the trees through the silvery atoms of air and the mysterious ether to the great moon.

If she went out in the dark for a drink of water from the troughs, or stepped across to the farm buildings to watch the milking, he was outside waiting to float along with her. Sometimes she raced along the Whitewell field to the distant barn just to see him race across the world.

He looked at her through the windows when she helped to shut the shutters, and he shone through the long latticed windows in the hall, making patterns on the barometer and high-backed chairs, lighting up the delicate carving as if a silver lamp hung there.

She never looked at him when he was new through glass, for he hated mirrors and windows until he was full grown, and she always bowed to him three times, as her mother had taught her. Never did she point a finger at him, for he would resent it, and one does not lightly incur the displeasure of the powerful moon. The moon was everybody's friend at Windystone, but no one talked to him and told him secrets and delightful plans as Susan did.

He saved candles and so saved money. Dan blew out his lamps as he came up the hills when the moon was out. Tea parties, occasional visits to other farms, Peacock Farm with its great rooms and remains of splendour, Daisy Bank Farm with its thatched barns and irregular garden and its pond with bulrushes, Greensleeve Farm built in the ruins of a monastery: none of these could be visited except when the moon would light the drive home, and aid the candles in the trap.

But where the moon went in between the visits Susan did not know. She asked Joshua about it.

'Tell me about the moon, Joshua,' she said coaxingly one night, as he sat making spelds for the candles. 'Was it just the same when you were a boy?'

'Well, it seems to be a deal smaller now, but I don't know. Like a man gets smaller when he's old. I've heeard tell the moon was once a part of the earth, and it always sort of hankers to get back, and pulls at it.'

'I do know this,' said Becky, looking up from her work, 'I do know there is a man in the moon, because I've seen him.'

'So have we all,' said Joshua, 'and he was taken up for picking sticks on Sunday, and his dog was took with him, too.'

'That's true,' said Becky, 'but it must be lonely up there for him.'

Susan hugged herself secretly. She knew him quite well, but he wasn't lonely now that *she* talked to him.

'You must never fell trees by moonlight, or they will rot away and be no good to nobody,' said Tom, 'and never let the moon shine on your scythe or on a looking-glass.'

'That reminds me, Becky, go and put out that cloth. Spread it on the grass plot for the moon to bleach,' said Margaret, who just came in. Becky went out and Susan with her to spread the stained cloth in the moonlight, where it lay all night.

Winter was the reign of moonlight and candles. Everyone had either one or the other to light them about the house and farm. Lamps were friends, but candles were jolly little comrades. A candle took Susan to bed, a white petticoated candle in a grey pewter candlestick with a rim of beads round the edge and an extinguisher hooked on the side. Her shadow ran up the stairs, and into the bedroom, where it played among the long pointed shadows of the bed.

Little hot drops of wax fell on her fingers and she rolled them into tiny balls and ranged them round the candlestick. A black stranger sat in the flame and she pushed him away. A winding sheet unfolded in stiffly starched ripples, and she hurriedly broke it off. A tiny puff of smoke fluttered off alone, and she knew she would have a surprise. A little red letter lay on the wick, but it would not be hers, the postman never brought a letter for Susan, it must be for her mother.

Upstairs, downstairs, in pantry, parlours, and dairy, ran little candles all the winter evenings, like glow-worms in the dark. They even went out of doors, sheltered in curving hands, when Becky went to the trough or Dan fetched the milk. When the lanterns were blown out, after milking, candles were used for everything, except when the moon was out to do his share of work.

The house was so high the moon had a good view of everything. He could stare in and run his fingers over the cupboards and china, and look at the pictures and laugh at and enjoy the things he saw.

He fetched Susan out of bed, right out to the lawn one night. She could not sleep. She heard the bolts shot and the locks turned and the soft thud of stockinged feet coming upstairs. Then bedroom doors shut and little lights flickered out through the windows. In a few minutes the house was quiet.

She crept from her bed and looked out of the window. A soft radiance flooded the fields making them white as snow. She shivered and got back to the warmth, but it was no good, she could feel the moon pulling her as it pulled the earth.

Down the creaking stairs she went, step by step, with her hand clutching the banister and her eyes wide as she met the glassy stare of the stuffed fox on the landing, alive and vigilant in the moonbeams.

She glided by her parents' door and heard a murmur of voices. She reached the hall and hesitated.

Should she go out by the front door or by the homely kitchen? She chose the front door, but the lock was too stiff for her fingers, and she slipped into the kitchen.

Mice scurried as she opened the door, and the room gasped with surprise. A glowing coal in the fire showed her the bull's-eye glass in the clock winking and alive. It understood and would come too if it could lift its heavy foot.

A feeling of a presence came upon her, as if the ghosts of all the Garlands who had lived there had been sitting chatting round the hearth, and now they stopped, surprised and breathless. She had nearly caught them this time, they said, as they leaned back waiting for her to go. The air trembled with their movements, and she waited for it to be still before she crossed the room and climbed on a chair to pull the long bolts and turn the heavy lock.

Then she stepped out under the sky. She ran down the little path to the wicket gate and lifted up her face.

'Here I am,' she whispered eagerly, and she thought of the infant Samuel. But no God was there, only the bright face of the moon, very near the earth; she felt she could touch him if she had a ladder.

She went out onto the lawn and stood with cold bare feet on the wet grass. The moon moved too, and stopped when she stopped.

Something rustled in the ivy bushes, perhaps a bird, moving in his sleep, tucking his head afresh under his wing. But she kept her eyes on the moon as if she were caught in a web hanging through the air, dipping down and up again, thinking of nothing, unconscious of time, surrendering herself to the flood of light. A great peace floated round her and happiness wrapped her.

She felt the earth swimming through space, as she had felt it before, swinging past the stars, on through the dark sky, and the moon came too. Never would she be lonely, even when she was quite old, she would have the moon, who would go with her. Even when she was dead, and she shot up, a shooting star, the moon would be up there too.

The quietness of the night became intense, she could hear her heart beating and she thought it was the earth's. She knew now that the earth was alive, the rocks were living beings, immortals were around her. So that was what the moon wanted to tell her.

The old house behind her seemed to stir and try to speak to her. She turned to it and stretched out a hand.

The moon slipped into a cloud like a fish into a net, and a shadow fell over the earth.

'Good night,' she whispered, 'everything,' and she went through the door into the dark house again.

She fastened the locks and bolts and crept, tired out, with eyes tightly shut, up the stairs. Her fingers traced the way, round corners to her high attic, where, with eyes still fast closed to keep in the secrets, she climbed into bed and fell asleep.

There were days of rain, when long slanting spears came stabbing through the air, beating down the grass, crashing against the windows. The farm was lost in the clouds, the men staggered through rushing streams, and wild winds blew them off their feet. Doors banged and windows rattled as if a devil were shaking their teeth out. The horses went about their work with streaming sides and bent heads, and Joshua and Tom walked sideways to the gale with sacks on their heads and shoulders.

Becky and Margaret wrapped themselves in cloaks when they went to the troughs or farm buildings, for umbrellas were useless in the hills. The passages were awash with rain carried in on drenched clothes.

Susan walked home with her feet little lumps of ice, dragged along by two bones. Her nose was a pink button, and her hair rat-tails. She was late and bedraggled because she could scarcely get through the pools in the wood, the trees had lashed and scratched her face. The matches were damp and she had no light, so she floundered along, bumping into outstretched boughs, tripping over stones and into wide pools.

She was undressed by the fire and wrapped up in a rug. She squatted on a three-legged, scarlet stool by the settle with her toes on the sanded hearth, and ate her plate of hot meat and vegetables, whilst the rain banged on the shutters like someone trying to get in.

'Hark, hark!' cried Becky with uplifted hand. 'They are outside, knocking. They want to come in. Hark!'

'Who is it?' asked Susan with wide-open eyes.

'It's the bad ones, as is dead,' whispered Becky in awed tones, and Susan crept nearer the oven door and was glad she was safe. The wind battered against the strong walls of the house, or prowled round corners, howling like a wolf waiting to leap when the door was opened.

There were thunderstorms and green lightning, which lit up the hills and woods, and made the men run for shelter. Tom warned them thunder was about, and soon it crashed with a thousand echoes. Susan enjoyed the brilliant lights and the rolling thunder which shook the wood and frightened all the evil things away. She walked slowly in order to see a thunderbolt drop like a ball of fire on the ground, or the trees split asunder over her head. But her mother was white with fear when she got in, and clasped her as if she were newly returned from the dead.

'It's God talking,' said Becky. 'He's angry with somebody.' But Susan's conscience was clear, and she had no qualms that she was the cause of the thunder and lightning. Her heart was hard again, hell had lost its terrors for a time, and she was filled with pagan delight and love for the earth.

CHAPTER 11

December

DECEMBER was a wonderful month. Jack Frost painted ferns and tropical trees with starry skies over the windows, hidden behind the shutters to surprise Becky when she came down in the morning.

'Look at the trees and stars he's made with his fingers,' she called to Susan, who ran from the kitchen to the parlour, and into the south parlour and dairy to see the sights. It really was kind of him to take all that trouble, and she saw him, a tall thin man with pointed face and ears, running round the outside of the house, dipping his long fingers in a pointed bag to paint on the glass those delicate pictures.

'Look at the feathers the Old Woman is dropping from the sky,' cried Becky, as she opened the door and looked out on a world of snow.

'They are not feathers, it's snow,' explained Susan impatiently. Really Becky didn't know everything.

'And what is snow but feathers,' returned Becky triumphantly. 'It's the Old Woman plucking a goose.'

Susan accepted it and gazed up to see the Old Woman, wide and spreading across the sky, with a goose as big as the world across her knees.

'Hark to the poor souls moaning,' Becky cried when the wind called sadly and piped through the cracks of the doors. 'That's the poor dead souls, crying there,' and she shivered whilst Susan stared out with grieved eyes, trying to pierce the air and see the shadowy forms wringing their hands and weeping for their lost firesides and warm blankets as they floated over the icy woods.

But at Christmas the wind ceased to moan. Snow lay

thick on the fields and the woods cast blue shadows across it.
The fir trees were like sparkling, gem-laden Christmas trees,
the only ones Susan had ever seen. The orchard, with the
lacy old boughs outlined with snow, was a grove of fairy
trees. The woods were enchanted, exquisite, the trees were
holy, and anything harmful had shrunken to a thin wisp and
had retreated into the depths.

The fields lay with their unevennesses gone and paths
obliterated, smooth white slopes criss-crossed by black lines
running up to the woods. More than ever the farm seemed
under a spell, like a toy in the forest, with little wooden
animals and men; a brown horse led by a stiff little red-
scarfed man to a yellow stable door; round, white, woolly
sheep clustering round a blue trough of orange mangolds;
red cows drinking from a square, white trough, and returning to a painted cow-house.

Footprints were everywhere on the snow, rabbits and
foxes, blackbirds, pheasants and partridges, trails of small
paws, the mark of a brush, and the long feet of the cock
pheasant and the tip-mark of his tail.

A jay flew out of the wood like a blue flashing diamond
and came to the grass-plot for bread. A robin entered the
house and hopped under the table whilst Susan sat very still
and her father sprinkled crumbs on the floor.

Rats crouched outside the window, peeping out of the
walls with gleaming eyes, seizing the birds' crumbs and
scraps, and slowly lolloping back again.

Red squirrels ran along the walls to the back door, close
to the window to eat the crumbs on the bench where the
milk cans froze. Every wild animal felt that a truce had come
with the snow, and they visited the house where there was
food in plenty, and sat with paws uplifted and noses
twitching.

For the granaries were full, it had been a prosperous year,
and there was food for everyone. Not like the year before
when there was so little hay that Tom had to buy a stack in
February. Three large haystacks as big as houses stood in the

stack-yard, thatched evenly and straight by Job Fletcher, who was the best thatcher for many a mile. Great mounds showed where the roots were buried. The brick-lined pit was filled with grains and in the barns were stores of corn.

The old brew-house was full of logs of wood, piled high against the walls, cut from trees which the wind had blown down. The coal-house with its strong ivied walls, part of the old fortress, had been stored with coal brought many a mile in the blaze of summer; twenty tons lay under the snow.

On the kitchen walls hung the sides of bacon and from hooks in the ceiling dangled great hams and shoulders. Bunches of onions were twisted in the pantry and barn, and an empty cow-house was stored with potatoes for immediate use.

The floor of the apple chamber was covered with apples, rosy apples, little yellow ones, like cowslip balls, wizened apples with withered, wrinkled cheeks, fat, well-fed, smooth-faced apples, and immense green cookers, pointed like a house, which would burst in the oven and pour out a thick cream of the very essence of apples.

Even the cheese chamber had its cheeses this year, for there had been too much milk for the milkman, and the cheese presses had been put into use again. Some of them were Christmas cheese, with layers of sage running through the middles like green ribbons.

Stone jars like those in which the forty thieves hid stood on the pantry floor, filled with white lard, and balls of fat tied up in bladders hung from the hooks. Along the broad shelves round the walls were pots of jam, blackberry and apple, from the woods and orchard, Victoria plum from the trees on house and barn, black currant from the garden, and red currant jelly, damson cheese from the half-wild ancient trees which grew everywhere, leaning over walls, dropping their blue fruit on paths and walls, in pigsty and orchard, in field and water trough, so that Susan thought they were wild as hips and haws.

Pickles and spices filled old brown pots decorated with

crosses and flowers, like the pitchers and crocks of Will Shakespeare's time.

In the little dark wine chamber under the stairs were bottles of elderberry wine, purple, thick, and sweet, and golden cowslip wine, and hot ginger, some of them many years old, waiting for the winter festivities.

There were dishes piled with mince pies on the shelves of the larder, and a row of plum puddings with their white calico caps, and strings of sausages, and round pats of butter, with swans and cows and wheat-ears printed upon them.

Everyone who called at the farm had to eat and drink at Christmastide.

A few days before Christmas Tom Garland and Dan took a bill-hook and knife and went into the woods to cut branches of scarlet-berried holly. They tied them together with ropes and dragged them down over the fields, to the barn. Tom cut a bough of mistletoe from the ancient hollow hawthorn which leaned over the wall by the orchard, and thick clumps of dark-berried ivy from the walls.

Indoors Mrs Garland and Susan and Becky polished and rubbed and cleaned the furniture and brasses, so that everything glowed and glittered. They decorated every room, from the kitchen where every lustre jug had its sprig in its mouth, every brass candlestick had its chaplet, every copper saucepan and preserving-pan had its wreath of shining berries  and leaves, through the hall, which was a bower of green, to the two parlours which were festooned and hung with holly and boughs of fir, and ivy berries dipped in red raddle, left over from sheep marking.

Holly decked every picture and ornament. Sprays hung over the bacon and twisted round the hams and herb bunches. The clock carried a crown on his head, and every dish-cover had a little sprig. Susan kept an eye on the lonely forgotten humble things, the jelly moulds and colanders and nutmeg-graters, and made them happy with glossy leaves. Everything seemed to speak, to ask for its morsel of greenery, and she tried to leave out nothing.

On Christmas Eve fires blazed in the kitchen and parlour and even in the bedrooms. Becky ran from room to room with the red-hot salamander which she stuck between the bars to make a blaze, and Margaret took the copper warming-pan filled with glowing cinders from the kitchen fire and rubbed it between the sheets of all the beds. Susan had come down to her cosy tiny room with thick curtains at the window, and a fire in the big fireplace. Flames roared up the chimneys as Dan carried in the logs and Becky piled them on the blaze. The wind came back and tried to get in, howling at the key-holes, but all the shutters were cottered and the doors shut. The horses and mares stood in the stables, warm and happy, with nodding heads. The cows slept in the cow-houses, the sheep in the open sheds. Only Rover stood at the door of his kennel, staring up at the sky, howling to the dog in the moon, and then he, too, turned and lay down in his straw.

In the middle of the kitchen ceiling there hung the kissing-bunch, the best and brightest pieces of holly made in the shape of a large ball which dangled from the hook. Silver and gilt drops, crimson bells, blue glass trumpets, bright oranges and red polished apples, peeped and glittered through the glossy leaves. Little flags of all nations, but chiefly Turkish for some unknown reason, stuck out like quills on a hedgehog. The lamp hung near, and every little berry, every leaf, every pretty ball and apple had a tiny yellow flame reflected in its heart.

Twisted candles hung down, yellow, red, and blue, unlighted but gay, and on either side was a string of paper lanterns.

Margaret climbed on a stool and nailed on the wall the Christmas texts, 'God bless our Home', 'God is Love',

'Peace be on this House', 'A Happy Christmas and a Bright New Year'.

Scarlet-breasted robins, holly, mistletoe, and gay flowers decorated them, and the letters were red and blue on a black ground. Never had Susan seen such lovely pictures, she thought, as she strained up and counted the number of letters in each text to see which was the luckiest one.

Joshua sat by the fire, warming his old wrinkled hands, and stooping forward to stir the mugs of mulled ale which warmed on the hob. The annual Christmas game was about to begin, but he was too old to join in it, and he watched with laughing eyes, and cracked a joke with anyone who would listen.

Margaret fetched a mask from the hall, a pink face with small slits for eyes through which no one could see. Then Becky put it on Dan's stout red face and took him to the end of the room, with his back to the others. Susan bobbed up and down with excitement and a tiny queer feeling that it wasn't Dan but somebody else, a stranger who had slipped in with the wind, or a ghost that had come out of the cob-webbed interior of the clock to join in the fun. She never quite liked it, but she would not have missed the excitement for anything.

Dan stood with his head nearly touching the low ceiling. His hair brushed against bunches of thyme and sage, and he scratched his face against the kissing-bunch, to Joshua's immense satisfaction and glee.

Becky and Susan and Margaret stood with their backs to the fire, and Tom lay back on the settle to see fair play.

'Jack, Jack, your supper's ready,' they called in chorus, chuckling and laughing to each other.

'Where's the spoon?' asked Dan, holding out his hands.

'Look all round the room,' they cried gleefully.

'Can't see it,' exclaimed Dan as he twisted his neck round to the shuttered windows, up to the kissing-bunch, and down to the floor.

'Look on top of All Saints' Church,' they sang.

Dan turned his mask up to the ceiling.

'Lump of lead,' he solemnly replied.

'Then catch them all by the hair of the head!' they shrieked, running and shouting with laughter.

Dan chased after them, tumbling over stools, catching the clock, hitting the row of coloured lanterns, pricking his neck, and walking into doors, cupboards, and dressers.

Susan ran, half afraid, but wholly happy, except when the pink mask came too near and the sightless eyes turned towards her, when she couldn't help giving a scream. Joshua warded him away from the flames, and Tom kept him from upsetting the brass and copper vessels which gleamed like fires under the ceiling.

Susan was caught by her hair and she became Jack. Now she put on the strange-smelling mask, and with it she became another person, bold, bad, fearless.

So it went on, the old country game, whilst Margaret kept stopping to peep in the oven at the mince pies and roast potatoes.

Next came 'Turn the Trencher', but Dan couldn't stop to play, for he had to be off a-guisering. He blacked his face with burnt cork and whitened his eyebrows. He borrowed Becky's black straw hat and wrapped her shawl round his shoulders. Then off he went to join a party of farm lads who were visiting the scattered farms.

He had not long been gone, and Tom was spinning the trencher between finger and thumb in the middle of the floor, when the dog barked as if someone were coming.

'Whist, whist,' cried old Joshua.

'Hark,' cried Tom, stopping the whirling board, 'there's something doing.'

They heard muffled steps coming down the path to the door.

'It's the guisers coming here,' cried Tom, and they all stood up expectantly with eager faces and excited whispers.

Here we come a-wassailing
Among the leaves so green,
Here we come a-wandering,
So fair to be seen.

We are not daily beggars
That beg from door to door,
But we are neighbours' children,
Whom you have seen before.

Call up the butler of this house,
Put on his golden ring,
Let him bring us up a glass of beer,
And better we shall sing.

Here they pushed open the door and half entered.

God bless the master of this house,
And bless the mistress, too,
And call the little children
That round the table go.

And all your kin and kinsfolk,
That dwell both far and near,
I wish you a Merry Christmas,
And a happy New Year.

'Come in, come in,' shouted Tom, with his broad face wreathed in smiles. Half a dozen young men and a woman stamped their feet and entered, bringing clots of snow and gusts of the sweet icy air. Their faces were masked and they disguised their voices, speaking in gruff tones or high falsettos, which caused much gay laughter.

They stood in a row in front of the dresser, and asked riddles of one another.

'How many sticks go to the building of a crow's nest?'

'None, for they are all carried.'

'When is a man thinner than a lath?'

'When he's a-shaving.'

'Who was the first whistler, and what tune did he whistle?'

'The wind, and he whistled "Over the hills and far away".'

'What is that which a coach cannot move without, and yet it's no use to it?'

'A noise.'

Tom and Joshua knew the answers and kept mum, but Becky and Susan were busy guessing, Margaret too.

Then Tom said, 'Now I'll give you one.

> *In a garden there strayed*
> *A beautiful maid, as fair as the flowers of the morn;*
> *The first hour of her life she was made a wife,*
> *And she died before she was born.'*

The guisers made wild guesses and Tom sat back, smiling and gleeful.

'No, you're wrong, it's Eve,' he said at last in a tone of triumph.

'And here's another,' he continued:

> *There is a thing was three weeks old,*
> *When Adam was no more;*
> *This thing it was but four weeks old,*
> *When Adam was four score.'*

The guisers gave it up, and Susan, who had heard it many a time, could scarcely keep the word within her mouth, but Tom frowned and nudged her to be quiet.

''Tis the moon,' he cried, and they all nodded their masks.

'Here's one,' said Joshua:

> *I've seen you where you never were,*
> *And where you ne'er will be;*
> *And yet within that very place,*
> *You shall be seen by me.'*

When they couldn't guess it and had murmured, 'You've seen me where I never was' many times, he told them, 'In a looking-glass'.

'Eh, Mester Taberner,' cried one. 'You've never seed me in a looking-glass,' and they all guffawed.

'And I know that voice,' returned Joshua, ''tis Jim Hodges from Over Wood way.'

'You're right, Mester Taberner,' said Jim, as he removed his mask and disclosed his red cheeks.

So the guessing went on, until all the mummers were unmasked, Dick Jolly, Tom Snow, Bob Bird, Sam Roper, and Miriam Webster.

They drew up chairs to the fire and Susan got plates and big china mugs, and the two-handled posset cups. Margaret piled the mince pies, as big as saucers, on a fluted dish and handed them round.

'Help yourselves, help yourselves, "Christmas comes but once a year, and when it comes it brings good cheer,"' said Tom, and he poured out the spiced hot ale for the men, and the women ate posset with nutmeg and sugar.

When the guisers had eaten and drunk, old Joshua rose to his feet to give them all his Christmas piece, 'The Mistletoe Bough'.

Susan listened to the poem she knew so well, repeating it after him under her breath. She knew that poor bride would get in the oak chest, there was no stopping her, but she felt thankful that when she herself went to bed it would be in the Little Chamber, and not alongside the fatal chest in the attic. But she loved to hear Joshua tell the story in his old cracked voice, which quavered when he was excited.

The guisers stamped in applause, and clapped their hands. They put on their masks, saying, 'He's got a rare memory,' and stood up to sing a last song.

Then, calling good wishes, greetings, blessings, tags of wit, they left the farm, and stumbled with lanterns and sticks across the fields to Oak Meadow.

'That Miriam should not go a-guisering with those men,' said Becky indignantly, when the door was shut, and they returned to the fire. 'She should think shame of herself.'

She flounced off to her own chair, by the dresser, for she and Dan never sat in the family circle.

''Tis an old custom, that,' observed Tom, as he leaned back against the comfortable cushions of the settle, 'but when my father was young and his father before him, they did a play, a mumming play, with no words.'

Then he told stories of his childhood, which Susan enjoyed more than anything, of Windystone in far-away days, when the dead-and-gone lived there. He told how they brewed their own beer in the brew-house, and made their tallow-dips. His grandmother sat in the chimney corner with a spinning-wheel, and made the very same cloth they had on the table. He told of the horse thief who stole the mare out of the orchard, and how he would have been hanged if they had caught him. He told of the mesmerists who gave enter-tainments in Raddle and Dangle, hypnotizing the people with passes of their hands so that they did whatever they were told. He told of the ghost his father met by the gate in the meadow, which never answered but brought death to the house. Strange, grim stories, which Susan would never forget.

'Tell the funny tale of the man who sold his wife,' she implored when Tom paused.

'There was a man, lived at Leadington, he went by the name of Abraham Maze. He couldn't get on with his wife.'

'Don't tell that tale before Susan,' interrupted Margaret indignantly.

'Why, what's the matter with it? There's no harm in it! It's a warning to cacklers,' and Tom looked round the company as if he accused them all.

'Well, as I was saying, he couldn't get on with his wife. She had such a tongue, it went nineteen to the dozen, never still a moment, clatter, clatter, clatter all day and night too. They led a regular cat-and-dog life, and she drove him to drink, although he was a steady fellow.

'Well, he was talking about her one night at the Pig with Two Faces, that's the name of the inn at Leadington, it's a farmhouse too. There's a sign of a pig with half its face laughing, as it might be, and half scowling.'

'Yes, I knows it,' said Joshua. 'I've been there many a time to lend a mare for their muck-carting. They were short of a horse.'

'Well,' continued Tom patiently, 'he told the folk about his wife, and everybody was right sorry for him, although they couldn't help laughing at him for being so hen-pecked. Then a stranger asks, "Will you sell her?"'

'So he says, "Right willing I will, if anyone wants to buy such truck."'

'Then it was very rude and wicked of him,' cried Margaret, 'to talk about his wife like that.'

'Will you be quiet?' Tom was exasperated. 'How can I tell a tale if you will keep interrupting? "How much do you want, Master?" asked the man.

' "Sixpence," shouts Maze, banging his fist on the table. "You can have her for sixpence, that's all she's worth."

' "Done," shouts the other fellow, "sixpence I'll give."

'So he paid the sixpence right there, and went home with Maze. She went away with the other man that very night. I forget his name, he was a Frenchy that bought her.'

'And what happened then?' asked Susan, wondering in her heart if anyone would sell her when she was grown up.

'She lived with him for a few weeks, and then ran away and went back to her first husband. And the funny thing was, he was glad to have her back again, to mend his stockings and cook.'

'Matrimony's a terrible queer thing,' said Joshua, and he shook his shoulders and felt in his pocket for his snuff-box, to clear his head.

'Matrimony and sorrow begins,' said Susan dreamily, 'matrimony and sorrow begins.' She did not know what the words meant, but she lifted up her young face to gaze into Joshua's deeply furrowed old cheeks, his thick white hair, and his tender mouth. He was thinking of his dead wife and the trouble he had had.

'Do you know what that is, Joshua?' she asked, putting her hand on his knee to wake him from his dream.

'I ought to know, Susan,' he replied.

'It's bread and butter, Joshua, with a piece of cake between. The bread and butter is sorrow, you know, and the cake is matrimony. I have it for tea when I'm good,' she explained.

'I used always to call it "Matrimony and Solla beggins",' she laughed.

'We've had both,' said Margaret, stroking her husband's hand, 'but we've not had the sorrow many people have had. We've a lot to be thankful for.'

The clock rattled its chain and took a deep loud breath as it drew itself up ready to strike. Then slowly, loudly, brooking no interfering conversation, it chimed nine o'clock, the last stroke singing on as if it were loath to leave the warm comfort of the dark cobwebbed interior, to venture out into the brightness of the kitchen and away through the keyhole and chimney, into the great lonely world beyond.

'In three hours it will be Christmas Day,' continued Margaret. 'The shepherds are out on the hillside, minding the sheep, and the star is shining in the sky. Get me the Bible, Susan, and I will read the chapter.'

Susan took the old brown leather Bible from the dresser where it lay ready for use by the spoon box, and laid it on the table in front of her mother, who searched among the little texts which lay within for the place.

Joshua and Tom sat up straight to listen, Susan drew her low chair to the fire, and Becky sat down in her correct place as servant at the bottom of the table.

The wind thumped at the door, so that the latch rattled, and cried sadly as it tried to get in to listen to the tale. The flames licked round the bars and held their breath as the old words dropped peacefully in the room.

'And it came to pass in those days that there went out a decree from Caesar Augustus that all the world should be taxed.'

Joseph and Mary went to Bethlehem on a dark night to pay their tax, and there was no room for them at the inn. How cold it was, snow everywhere, and perhaps wolves prowling round, thought Susan, as the wind howled under the kitchen door. They walked up and down, up and down, till they found a stable, and she thought of them walking across the fields stumbling against rocks and trees, in deep snow, to the stable in the cobbled yard underneath the weathercock.

There Jesus was born and put in the manger. The ox and the ass stood watching and Joseph had a lantern to look at the little Baby Boy. But afar in a field some shepherds were minding their sheep and they saw a star. Susan knew which one it was, it shone through the fir tree across the lawn.

The star moved, just as the moon moved when it brought her home through the wood in winter, and the shepherds left their sheep and followed it.

The sheep were not lonely that night because it was like day with that big bright star in the sky, and a host of angels floated in the air, singing, 'Glory to God in the Highest, and on earth peace, goodwill toward men.' The sheep stopped eating to look up at the angels, but they were not afraid.

The shepherds followed the star till it came above the stable, and there it stopped, in the branches of the elm tree. The stable door was open, and the little horseshoe in the upper door shone in the starlight, and the brighter light from within came streaming out to meet them. It was warm inside, with hay and the animals' breath, so the Baby and Mary sat cosily in the manger. Mary's feet were tucked up so that she could get in with the Holy Child, and bits of hay and straw were sticking to her blue dress.

Susan could scarcely keep the tears from her eyes, she was so excited over the story she knew so well. If only she had been there too, a little girl with those shepherds, she would have seen the Wise Men ride up on their camels, through the gate into the yard. They carried gold and frankincense and myrrh, yellow gold as big as a lump of coal, and myrrh like leaves, smelling sweeter than lavender or mignonette, and frankincense, something, she didn't know what, something in a blue and gold box with red stones on it.

Then Mrs Garland put a little embroidered cross in the Bible and closed its pages reverently. She took off her spectacles and laid them on the table, and they all knelt down to pray.

They prayed for the Queen and Country, for the three doves, Peace, Wisdom, and Understanding, and they thanked God for all the blessings of this life.

But Susan's head began to nod, and she rested it on the hard chair. When the others arose, she still knelt there, fast asleep.

So her mother roused her, and she said 'Good night, God bless you,' for anyone might disappear in the night, and they went upstairs together to the Little Chamber, where a fire burned in the grate, and shadows jumped up and down the ceiling, fire-shadows the best of all.

She hung up her stocking at the foot of the bed and fell asleep. But soon singing roused her, and she sat up, bewildered. Yes, it was the carol-singers.

Margaret came running upstairs and wrapped her in a blanket. She took her across the landing to her own room, and pulled up the linen blind.

Outside under the stars she could see the group of men and women with lanterns throwing beams across the paths and on to the stable door. One man stood apart beating time, another played a fiddle, and another had a flute. The rest sang in four parts the Christmas hymns, 'While Shepherds watched', 'Come all ye Faithful', and 'Hark, the herald angels sing'.

There was the star, Susan could see it twinkling and bright in the dark boughs with their white frosted layers, and there was the stable. She watched the faces half lit by the lanterns, top-coats pulled up to their necks. The music of the violin came thin and squeaky, like a singing icicle, blue and cold, but magic, and the flute was warm like the voices.

They stopped and waited a moment. Tom's deep voice came from the darkness. They trooped, chattering and puffing out their cheeks, and clapping their arms round their bodies to the front door. They were going into the parlour for elderberry wine and their collection money. A bright light flickered across the snow as the door was flung wide open. Then a bang, and Susan went back to bed.

Christmas Eve was nearly over, but tomorrow was Christmas Day, the best day in all the year. She shut her eyes and fell asleep.

CHAPTER 12

Christmas Day

SUSAN awoke in the dark of Christmas morning. A weight lay on her feet, and she moved her toes up and down. She sat up and rubbed her eyes. It was Christmas Day. She stretched out her hands and found the knobby little stocking, which she brought into bed with her and clasped tightly in her arms as she fell asleep again.

She awoke later and lay holding her happiness, enjoying the moment. The light was dim, but the heavy mass of the chest of drawers stood out against the pale walls, all blue like the snowy shadows outside. She drew her curtains and looked out at the starry sky. She listened for the bells of the sleigh, but no sound came through the stillness except the screech owl's call.

Again she hadn't caught Santa Claus. Of course she knew he wasn't real, but also she knew he was. It was the same with everything. People said things were not alive but you knew in your heart they were: statues which would catch you if you turned your back were made of stone; Santa Claus was your own father and mother; the stuffed fox died long ago.

But suppose people didn't *know*! They hadn't seen that stone woman walk in Broomy Vale Arboretum, but she might, in the dark night. They hadn't seen Santa Claus and his sleigh, but that was because they were not quick enough. Susan had nearly caught things happening herself, she knew they only waited for her to go away. When she looked through a window into an empty room, there was always a guilty look about it, a stir of surprise.

Perhaps Santa Claus had left the marks of his reindeer

and the wheels of his sleigh on the snow at the front of the house. She had never looked because last year there was no snow, and the year before she had believed in him absolutely. She would go out before breakfast, and perhaps she would find two marks of runners and a crowd of little hoof-marks.

She pinched the stocking from the toe to the top, where her white suspender tapes were stitched. It was full of nice knobs and lumps, and a flat thing like a book stuck out of the top. She drew it out – it *was* a book, just what she wanted most. She sniffed at it, and liked the smell of the cardboard back with deep letters cut in it. She ran her fingers along like a blind man and could not read the title, but there were three words in it.

Next came an apple, with its sweet, sharp odour. She recognized it, a yellow one, from the apple chamber, and from her favourite tree. She took a bite with her strong, white little teeth and scrunched it in the dark.

It was delicious fun, all alone, in this box-like room, with the dim blue-and-white jug on the washstand watching her, and the pool of the round mirror hanging on the wall, reflecting the blue dark outside, and the texts, 'Thou God seest Me', and 'Blessed are the Peacemakers', and 'Though your sins be as scarlet they shall be white as wool'. They could all see the things although she couldn't, and they were glad.

Next came a curious thing, pointed and spiked, with battlements like a tower. Whatever could it be? It was smooth like ivory and shone even in the dark. She ran her fingers round the little rim and found a knob. She gave it a tug, and a ribbon flew out – it was a tape-measure to measure a thousand things, the trees' girths, the calf's nose, the pony's tail. She put it on her knee and continued her search.

There was a tin ball that unscrewed and was filled with comfits, and an orange, and a sugar mouse, all these were easy to feel, a sugar watch with a paper face and a chain of coloured ribbon, a doll's chair, and a penny china doll with a round smooth head. She at once named it Diana, after Diana of the Ephesians, for this one could never be an idol, being made of pot. She put her next to her skin down the neck of her nightdress, and pulled the last little bumps out of the stocking toe. They were walnuts, smelling of the orchards at Bird-in-Bush Farm, where they grew on great trees overhanging the wall, and a silver shilling, the only one she ever got, and very great wealth, but it was intended for the money-box in the hall. It was the nicest Christmas stocking she had ever had, and she hugged her knees up to her chin and rocked with joy. Then she put her hand under her pillow and brought out five parcels which had made five separate lumps under her head. They were quite safe.

She heard the alarm go off in her father's room and Dan's bell go jingle-jangle. Five o'clock, plenty of time yet before the hoof-marks would disappear. The wind swished softly against the window, and thumps and thuds sounded on the stairs. She slept again with the doll on her heart and the tape-measure under her cheek and the book in her hand.

She was awakened again by the rattle of milk-cans below her window. Joshua and Becky were coming back with the milk, and it really was Christmas Day. All else was strangely silent, for the deep snow deadened the sound of footsteps. She jumped out of bed, pressed her nose against the window, and rubbed away the Jack Frost pictures. Everything was blue, and a bright star shone. From a window in the farm buildings a warm gleam fell on the snow. Dan was milking the last cow by the light of the lantern which hung on the wall.

Then she heard his cheerful whistle and the low moo of the cows as he came out with the can.

What had the cattle done all night? Did they know it was Christmas? Of course, all God's creatures knew. Becky said the cows and horses knelt down on Christmas Eve. She could see them going down on their front knees, the cows so easily, the horses so painfully, for their legs were wrong.

Sheep knelt when they had foot-rot, it would be easy for them. But down they all went, bowing to the New Saviour as she bowed to the new moon.

She washed in the basin with blue daisies round the rim, but she could see neither water nor soap. Candles were for night, not morning use. She brushed her hair in front of the ghost of a mirror, where a white little face looked like a flower-in-the-night. She slipped the round comb through her hair and put on her Sunday honey-combed dress with seven tucks in the skirt and two in the sleeves, a preparation for a long and lanky Susan.

Then she buttoned her slippers and said her short morning prayer, and down she tripped with her stocking-load of presents and the five parcels. She walked boldly past the fox and went to the landing window that overlooked the grass plots and lawn. The beeches were still, the apple trees stood blue and cream against the white hills, and there was a thin moon like a cow's horn in the trees.

She went into the hall and turned away from the closed kitchen door, where all was bustle, the noise of milk-cans, the roar of the fire, and the chatter of voices. The front door was unlocked and she lifted the heavy iron catch and slipped out into the virgin snow, blue and strange in the early light.

She lifted her feet high and walked to the gate in the wall surrounding the house. The monkey tree held out its arms to her, and she waved a hand. She crossed the walk and looked over the low stone wall at the lawn. There was no doubt something had been there in the night, footprints, but not hoof-marks, a fox, maybe, or a dog visiting Roger.

She returned to the house, shivering with delight, and opened the kitchen door. She was wrapped in colour and light, in sweet smells of cows and hay and coldness, brought in by the men, and new milk and hot sausages, tea and toast, warmth and burning wood from the hearth. The strongest smell was cold, which rushed through the back door sweeping all the other smells away, until the doors banged and the flame of the fire shot out.

'A merry Christmas, a merry Christmas,' she called, kissing everybody except Dan, which wouldn't be proper. 'Merry' was the word Susan liked, not the limp word, 'happy'.

She presented her paper parcels all round and sat down on the settle to watch the different faces. Dan opened his quickly in the passage and took out a pencil. He licked the point, wrote on the back of his hairy hand, stuck it behind his ear, and grinned his thanks as he went off with his churn.

Becky had a pen-wiper, made out of a wishing-bone and a piece of Margaret's black skirt, and a quill pen cut from a goose feather.

'Just what I wanted,' she cried nobly, for she didn't write a letter once a year, the reason being that she couldn't.

Old Joshua had a tiny bottle of scent, 'White Heather'.

'Thank you kindly, Susan,' said he, as he held up the minute bottle between his big finger and thumb, and struggled with the infinitesimal cork which was too small for him to grip. 'It will come in handy when I clean out the cows.'

To her mother she gave a text, painted by herself, and framed in straw and woolwork.

'O Death, where is thy sting? Where, Grave, thy Victory?'

She had spent many secret hours making this, and she looked anxiously to see what her mother thought of it.

A flicker passed over Mrs Garland's face as she kissed her cheek.

'It's very beautiful, my dear. Why did you choose the text?'

'Because it made me think of summer, of bees and wasps,' replied Susan with a joyful smile.

Her father's present was a big blue handkerchief with his initials embroidered in the corner, T.G.

Then Becky brought from out of the copper tea-urn a string of blue glass beads which she had bought for Susan at Mellow and hidden for months. Mrs Garland gave her a work-box like a house whose roof lifted off and inside there lay little reels of black and white cotton and a tin thimble. And, most startling, the chimney was a red velvet pin-cushion!

But Joshua's present was the most wonderful. It was nothing else than the purse with mother-of-pearl sides and red lining which she had seen at Broomy Vale and coveted so long. A miracle!

Susan displayed her stocking whilst they had breakfast. She was secretly rather disappointed over the book, which was called *Three Wet Sundays*. It was obviously a Sunday book, she had only *Pilgrim's Progress* and the Bible to read on Sundays, so it was a change, but it seemed to be about some children who talked of nothing but the Israelites for three wet Sundays.

When it was wet at Windystone she played with the Noah's Ark, that blessed present of three years ago, still as good as new through being kept for Sundays only. The stags had not lost their antlers, nor the cows their horns. The spotted dogs and blue calves were just as exciting. A camel had lost his leg and walked on a matchstick, and an ostrich had broken its beak, and the ducks and swans were pale through so much swimming, but Noah and all his relations were in the best of health, and slept in their matchbox beds or sent the dove from the window or looked after the guinea-pigs which were as big as dogs.

What a book that would have made, *Three Wet Sundays in Noah's Ark*!

The postman came through the wood with a bundle of letters and Christmas cards. He stood by the fire and had a cup of tea, and admired the decorations whilst Margaret opened her letters with cries of happiness, and excitement. She didn't stop to read them, she took out all the cards which had no names on them and popped them into envelopes. Then she readdressed them, dexterously re-shuffling and redealing, so that the postman should take them with him, a thrifty procedure.

Susan had a card which she liked above everything, a

church with roof and towers and foreground covered in glittering snow. But when it was held up to the light, colours streamed through the windows, reds and blues, from two patches at the back. She put it with her best treasures to be kept for ever.

It was nearly time to start for church and all was bustle and rush as usual. Margaret dressed herself in her plum-coloured merino trimmed with velvet, and dived under the bed for the bonnet-box from which she took her best bonnet and the sealskin muff. It was always wrapped up in a linen handkerchief with a sprig of lavender and lad's love, it was so precious.

Susan dragged on her brown coat running downstairs as she pulled at the sleeves, and her beaver hat with silky pom-poms at the side. She wanted to kiss her father once more under the kissing-bunch before she went.

Then everybody began to run, last-minute directions about the turkey and the stuffing, hunts for threepenny-bits, for Prayer Books, for handkerchiefs and lozenges, Joshua bumping into Susan's hat, Becky letting the milk boil over, Tom shouting, 'You'll be late again, and Christmas morning', and Susan running to play 'Christians awake' in the parlour, at the last minute, but they got off before the bells began to ring.

Down the hill they went, Mrs Garland first, Susan walking in her tracks, through the clean snow, like the page in 'Good King Wenceslas', along the white roads unmarked except by the hoofs and wheels of the milk carts, to the tune of gay dancing bells to the ivy-covered church.

Inside it was warm and beautiful, with ivy and holly, and lovely lilies and red leaves from the Court. The rich people wore their silks and furs, all scented and shining. Susan looked at them and wondered about their presents. She had heard they had real Christmas trees, with toys and candles like the one in *Hans Andersen*, which stood up in a room nearly to the ceiling. She would just like to peep at one for a minute, one minute only, to see if her imagination was right.

She was almost too happy, and her heart ached with joy as she stood on a hassock by her mother's side, with her hymn-book in her hand, singing 'Noel, Noel', feasting her eyes on the coloured windows and bright berries and flowers, wrapped in scents and sounds as in a cloud of incense. She buried her face in her muff in ecstasy. No thoughts of hell or idols today, only of Baby Jesus in the manger, and the singing angels.

It was over, they went out into the sweet air, with music pouring from the organ loft, and choir-boys scrambling out of their surplices. The river ran swiftly by, with edges of ice. The yew trees spread their long branches over the white graves. Poor dead, did they know it was Christmas? Susan felt she would like to lay a present on every grave, an apple and an orange, and she looked round with interest to see the reds and yellows in the snow. She nearly ran into a gleaming silk dress, only half covered by a mantle.

Why did it stand out all by itself, like that? How did it make that lovely noise, shir-r-r, shir-r-r, like the scythe cutting down nettles?

She put out a finger and touched the ruby silk. It was colder than her own wool frock, like a dock-leaf.

Mrs Garland had stopped to speak to someone, and Susan walked on silently in the snow, absorbed in the softness of silk and the loneliness of the dead.

It was Mrs Drayton's dress she had touched, and she was the mother of the girls with shining hair. They had a Christmas tree, the governess had told Mrs Garland. She must be very happy today, and Susan pressed close to her to smell the happiness.

'What a very plain child that Garland child is! Positively ugly,' said Mrs Drayton to her husband.

Susan gasped and stood still. The world was filled with sorrow. The gleaming snow was dulled, a cloud swept over the sun and the sky drooped.

Mrs Drayton turned round and saw the girl's startled eyes.

'Will you please ask your mother to send two shillings' worth of eggs?' she said stiffly, and passed on like a queen.

'I do hope that child did not hear what you said,' exclaimed Mr Drayton nervously, for he was continually embarrassed by his wife's loud remarks.

'It will do her good,' replied Mrs Drayton calmly; 'those Garlands are too independent.'

Susan dropped behind; her heart ached and lay heavy in her breast. She didn't mind being called 'plain', but 'ugly' was like the toad, rough-skinned and venomous, which walked round the garden, or the old witch at Dangle. She was numbed by the pain.

Her mother came hurrying up and together they walked through the crisp snow by the black river, frothing over large stones in cascades of spangles, like the lustres in Aunt Harriet's sitting-room. White boughs dipped curious fingers in the water, and gathered ice in the quiet pools. From a rock by the roadside long icicles hung, and as Susan looked at them she forgot her sorrow. There was beauty, and she climbed up to pick them, and carried them delicately in her fingers to preserve them.

She wouldn't be sad, she didn't care if she were ugly; she had accepted her wistful elfin face as she accepted the birds and trees, as something which was part of the earth.

Ice crackled under her boots as she walked along the frozen puddles and cleared away the snow with her toe. Below the surface she could see leaves and grass imprisoned like a ship in a bottle, like the soul in a man.

Mrs Garland sent thoughts running first up the hill, little servants, to make the bread-sauce, set the table with the best dinner service, pour out elderberry wine, and baste the turkey.

Susan dragged behind, peeping at the landscape through the icicle, watching her shadow move on the snow, climb little trees and slide up walls. A friendly thing a shadow is, neither ugly nor unkind, a fantastic dancing friend.

They climbed the hill and stopped at the first gate. There

was the square church tower, far away, with turrets like little black trees growing on the corners, and above it hung all the hymns and prayers, a bunch of white clouds.

There lay the great mass of Eve's Court with little spires of soft blue smoke coming from many chimneys, like the gentle breath from a dragon's many mouths. Susan pictured the cooks and kitchen-maids, with butler and footmen, racing round, piling wood on the fires, roasting pheasants and turkeys and geese, great sirloins and haunches of venison, carrying silver dishes of jellied moulds, rainbow colour, and golden fruits, to a vast dining-room where guests sat in high-backed chairs under the shade of a Christmas tree, glittering with candles and toys.

Her own chimneys were smoking, too, blue and grey against the clear sky, and Becky was running in and out of the kitchen with the basting-spoon in one hand and the flour-dredger in the other. She would far rather be on her high hill among her own treasures than down there in the valley, with the great ones of the earth.

She suddenly remembered the message.

'Mrs Drayton wants two shillings' worth of eggs, mother.'

'Did she mention it today? On Christmas Day? She shouldn't order eggs on Christmas Day,' cried Mrs Garland indignantly. 'I always knew she was no lady.'

There! Susan was vindicated. Of course Mrs Drayton wasn't one of the gentry, Eve's Court never called on her, everyone knew that, but she was no lady either, so she couldn't know whether Susan was ugly or not.

Susan had an infallible test for ladies. No lady turned round when she had passed. Often she had walked backwards for a mile or two, when she had been to Mellow on an errand, to see who turned round and who walked straight past with unseeing eyes. There were very few ladies, they all turned round to look at the little girl in the grey cape, who dawdled and twisted her lonely way along the road.

There was some secret abroad, Susan felt it as soon as they got in, by the odd silence, and the knowing glances she intercepted between Joshua and her father. The house tingled with it.

'Susan, go into the parlour and bring out my concertina,' said Tom, when Susan had put her gloves and Prayer Book in the bureau in the hall, and hung up her hat.

'What do you want a concertina now for, Tom?' asked Mrs Garland astonished, but such a flock of winks and nods flew about the room, she followed Susan across the hall.

'Mind it doesn't bite you,' called Tom.

In the middle of the table was a Christmas tree, alive and growing, looking very much surprised at itself, for had not Tom dug it up from the plantation whilst they were at church, and brought it in with real snow on its branches? The rosiest of apples and the nicest yellow oranges were strung to its boughs, and some sugar biscuits with pink icing and a few humbugs from Tom's pocket lay on the snow, with a couple of gaily coloured texts and a sugar elephant. On the top of the tree shone a silver bird, a most astonishing silver glass peacock with a tail of fine feathers, which might have flown in at the window, he wouldn't say Nay and he wouldn't say Yea.

Susan was amazed. If an angel from heaven had sat on the table she would have been less surprised. She ran to hug everybody, her heart was full.

They had been so busy getting ready, for Tom only thought of it when Dan was telling him the station gossip of Mrs Drayton's Christmas tree, they had neglected the dinner.

'Dang it,' Tom had said, 'we will have a Christmas tree, too. Go and get the spade, Dan.'

The ground had been like iron, the tree had spreading roots, but they had not harmed the little thing, and it was going back again to the plantation when Christmas was over.

The turkey was not basted, and the bread-sauce was forgotten, but everyone worked with a will and soon all was ready and piping hot.

The potatoes were balls of snow, the sprouts green as if they had just come from the garden, as indeed they had, for they too had been dug out of the snow not long before. The turkey was brown and crisp, it had been Susan's enemy for many a day, chasing her from the poultry-yard, and now it was brought low; the stuffing smelled of summer and the herb garden in the heat of the sun.

As for the plum pudding with its spray of red berries and shiny leaves and its hidden sixpence, which would fall out, and land on Susan's plate, it was the best they had ever tasted. There was no dessert, nor did they need it, for they sipped elderberry wine mixed with sugar and hot water in the old pointed wine-glasses, and cracked the walnuts damp from the trees.

Mrs Garland, with an air of mystery, brought out *her* surprise which had lain in the parlour bedroom a few days. It was a parcel from Susan's godmother, Miss Susanna Dickory.

Tom and Susan stooped over as Mrs Garland untied the string and put it carefully in the string bag. It didn't do to be impatient, there was plenty of time.

There was a red shawl which Miss Dickory's old fingers had knitted for Margaret, and a grey woollen muffler and gloves to match for Tom, also knitted by Miss Dickory, and *Uncle Tom's Cabin* for Susan.

'Well, she is kind,' said Margaret, 'she must have worked for weeks at those things. How useful! Mind you wear those gloves, Tom. I am glad I sent her that ham. You see I was right, Tom.'

'Yes,' agreed Tom, 'but you need not have sent a ham to Aunt Harriet, too. She never sends anything to us. It takes all our profit.'

'Cast your bread upon the water,' replied Margaret, and Susan looked up from the book which would soon entwine itself in her life and in her dreams. She pondered what it might mean. She never dare throw bread away, and her mother was the last person in the world to send loaves and ham floating down the river. Then she returned to the book in which she lost herself, lying before the parlour fire, until the dusk crept into the room and the firelight was insufficient even when she leaned into the fireplace.

Outside the world was amazingly blue, light blue snow, indigo trees, deep blue sky, misty blue farm and haystacks, and men with lanterns and bundles of hay on their backs for the horses and cows, or yokes across their shoulders as they went milking. Susan could hear Joshua breaking the ice on the trough by the edge of the lawn, and Duchess stood by his side waiting to drink. She lowered her great head, drank, looked around and savoured the delicious spring water on her tongue, then drank again, with snorts and soft grunts. She lifted her head and shook her mane, sending the loose drops from her muzzle in a shower round her.

Then she whinnied contentedly and walked halterless back to the stable, lowering her head as she went under the doorway, stepping carefully up the sill. The sounds of the rope and stone weight which tethered her could be heard, as Joshua fastened her up, and then he brought out Fanny, clattering her hoofs on the floor before they were silenced in the snow.

Yellow stars like lamps, blue stars like icicles, twinkled up above and far away across the valley. A running star showed a cart or gig travelling along the coach road to Mistchester, where the cathedral stood, and the big cattle market and fine shops.

Susan pressed her nose to the cold window-pane until it became a flat white button, and her breath froze into feathery crystals. 'This is Christmas Day, it's Christmas Day, it won't come again for a whole year. It's Christmas,' she murmured.

The blue deepened and Becky came in to set the tea.

'Shut the shutters, Susan, and keep out the cold. You'll be fair starved by that window. They'll soon be back from milking, and I'm going to chapel tonight. I've not been for many a long bit.'

Susan climbed on the leather-seated chairs and drew the

folded shutters out of their niches in the depths of the walls. She racketed them across the windows, with a last long look at the deepening blue, and dropped the iron bars into the clamps.

Then she ran to the other rooms, sending out the deep clang through the shadows, which always meant cosiness and home and fireside to those within.

But outside was the wonderful Christmas night with all its mysteries, its angels busy under the stars, and seraphs singing up in Paradise.

The men rattled through the kitchen with foaming pails, for the milk did not take long to cool in the biting air which froze the drops of moisture on Joshua's whiskers, and left Tom's hands stiff and white. They stamped their feet and left great paddocks of snow on the mats by the doors and in the passage.

The mare whinnied outside the shuttered windows, as Joshua led her out, with the thick yellow and red rug across her loins. Roger barked as the churns were silently rolled through thick snow, and lifted on the cart. Joshua cried, 'Coom up, lass,' and led her forward, and Tom fastened the pins in the hinged back. Susan made the milk tickets, Becky polished the lamp, and Dan drank a brimming mug of tea, and hurried out into the cold night, down the deep snowy hill. He led the mare and carried a small axe in his hand with which he knocked out the great clumps of clinging snow and ice which collected in her hoofs, causing her to stumble and slip. One fall and the milk would be upset, which had happened before now.

Becky had her tea alone in the kitchen before the fire, but old Joshua was invited to the parlour, to the feast.

There was Christmas cake, iced and sprinkled over with red and blue 'hundreds and thousands', with a paper flag in the middle, on one side of which was the Union Jack and on the other a clown with red nose and pointed hat, like the ones at the circus.

There was a fragrant ham, brother to those hanging in the

kitchen corner, smoked and delicately flavoured, under its coat of brown raspings, and its paper frill which Susan had cut the night before.

There was a pie stuffed with veal, ham and eggs, potted meats in china dishes with butter on the top, brown boiled eggs in the silver egg-stand which stood like a castle with eight stalwart egg-cups and eight curling spoons round the tall handle, white bread and butter on the Minton china plates with their tiny green leaves and gold edges, a pot of honey and strawberry jam, and an old Staffordshire dish of little tarts containing golden curds made of beastings, mixed with currants.

The green and white china cups which had belonged to Mrs Garland's grandmother were ranged at one end, beside the large teapot with its four little legs, the china sugar basin with its lid over real crystal lumps, not brown demerara as it was Christmas, the milk jug to match, and an ancient worn silver cream jug, the 'Queen Annie jug', full of thick cream which would scarcely pour out.

In the middle of the table were four silver candlesticks which were used on festal days instead of the lamp, holding four tall wax candles.

The delicate cups were passed up and down the table, the tiny plates heaped with food, Becky ran in and out with clean plates, knives and forks, with familiar jokes and smiles, as she filled up the dishes. Old Joshua ate enough for three, and then asked for more. The Christmas tree shone in the corner, and on the fire blazed a log which Becky could hardly lift when she carried it in.

The room was filled with brightness and laughter, even the shadows danced and flitted across the ceiling, four at a time, in country bobs and jigs.

They heard the sound outside of the returning cart just as the feast finished and Susan had said Grace. A piled plate with a little of everything was put ready for Dan, and Becky cleared away. Tom Garland stretched himself in the grandfather chair at one side of the fire, with his feet on the brass fender, and Joshua went out to help with the mare.

Becky washed up and cleared away before she got ready for chapel and Margaret wiped her precious china tenderly, with loving fingers and little reminiscences of when it had been used, weddings, funerals, birthdays, and Christmases.

Then Tom roused himself from his contemplation of the fire and came out to reach down the best lantern and get it ready. It hung between the old pointed horn lantern and Susan's little school lantern, a black shining case with cut-glass sides and a clean fine window at the front. He opened the back and put in a fresh piece of candle from the candle bark, and lit it.

The three set out with muffs, cloaks, walking-sticks, Prayer Books and Bibles, hymn-books, lozenges, clean hand-kerchiefs folded neatly, the lantern, and three pairs of old woollen stocking legs which they pulled over their boots to keep themselves from slipping. And even then Susan had to run back for the matches.

Becky walked in front with the lantern and a stick, Susan came next, and Mrs Garland last.

There was a great conversation and warnings of snow-drifts, for the snow had fallen again in the afternoon, and the path fell away on either side so that a false step would mean a drop into the cutting down which the horse and cart had fumbled their way in deeper snow.

The lantern gave a wavering light, for Becky shook and waddled in her walk, and shadows danced about on every side. The gorse bushes which had disappeared under the drifts lay in wait for legs and ankles, and snow cluttered the uplifted skirts and petticoats.

Susan loved every moment, but Margaret and Becky were thankful when at last they reached the bottom of the long slippery hill and they had the level road in front of them.

Becky flashed her lamp over the wall, fingers of light pointing to the dark river running on its secret business, talking incessantly to itself, aloof and incomprehensible.

They trudged along the turnpike, which was empty and lonely, past the milestones and the water mill, by wall and hedge, alike in the covering of snow. The church bells rang triumphantly, clear and pulsating in the stillness, racing, tumbling over one another, echoing in the hills, and then almost silent as they turned a corner and the bending river drowned the notes, or a mass of rock deflected it away. Sometimes they even caught a few notes of the bells at Brue-on-the-Water, a village far away across the hills in another valley.

In the woods above them they heard the bark of a fox. 'A heathen he is,' said Becky. 'He should know better than to be abroad tonight,' but Margaret told her foxes couldn't know, they had no souls.

The lights streamed from the church windows, straight across the graveyard, and in reds and blues the crucified Christ hung there.

'But He doesn't know about that yet,' thought Susan. 'He's only just born, a Baby a day old. I know more than He knows. I know He will be crucified and He doesn't know yet.'

It was a disturbing thought, which shattered her as she crunched the snow under her feet and stumbled along under the church walls. She wondered if she could warn Him, tell Him to go back to Heaven, quick, before He was caught by Judas. But of course she couldn't!

It was like Charles I. She always wanted to stop him, to save him from doing the fatal things which would surely lead him, which did lead him, to the block. She was caught up in time, the present slipped behind the past. But the bells were going ting tong, ting tong, in a great hurry, as if they wanted to be quick so that they could have a Christmas mystery of their own in the sky, to count the prayers floating out of the roof and watch the cherubim catch them in their nets and carry them off to Heaven.

Becky turned away at the lych-gate, and went on to chapel where there was no jumping up and down all the time like an ill-sitting hen, but folks could lean forward with their faces in their hands and have done with it.

They blew out the lantern and took the stockings off their boots, and hid them under the stone seat in the porch.

Susan took deep sniffs, as she stood for a moment by the red baize door, of hair-oil, lavender, comfortable warm stuffs, leather leggings, paraffin and peppermint, homely smells which welcomed her in.

The lights dazzled their eyes as they walked up the aisle, Margaret gliding quietly to her place, Susan tiptoeing behind her. Lamps hung from the walls and every dark holly leaf was a candle, every scarlet berry a farthing dip. The windows alone had lost their radiance, and stood back behind the colour and warmth which filled the church, almost visible to the child's eyes searching the air for invisible things, for God on the altar, and angels floating above the choir, for music beating its wings in the high dark beams of the roof, and for goodness and mercy running hand-in-hand down the chancel.

The service was different from the morning service, too. Everybody sang mightily, the deep voices of the old men and the tiny piping voices of children overpowering the organ and compelling it to a slow grandeur in 'While shepherds watched', and 'Hark! the herald angels sing', and 'Lead, kindly light'. They wouldn't be hurried for anyone, and Samuel Robinson must slacken his pace, going on as if he wanted to catch a train!

The old words rang out bravely, and the scent of bear's grease and peppermint balls filled the air like incense.

Susan was squeezed against her mother, close to that silky muff and the warm hand within it, by portly Mrs Chubb, who smiled and nodded and tinkled the bugles on her mantle, and shone like a crystal chandelier, besides smelling most deliciously of pear drops, which she passed to Susan when she knelt down to pray.

But the end was coming, they sang a carol, and knelt a few minutes in silence. Margaret poured out her heart to

God, asking His help in the thousand anxieties which lay before her, the winter and its dangers, spring and the birds, the harvest, and Susan knelt wrapped in the beauty of the season, thinking of the Christ-Child.

Then the villagers rose to their feet and passed out of church, to greet each other in the porch and find their mufflers, sticks, and pattens. Margaret lighted the lantern and they pulled their stockings over their shoes in the confusion of the crowd. Becky waited for them at the gate, and they called, 'Good night, good night. A happy Christmas and many of them. A happy Christmas and a prosperous New Year when it comes. Same to you and many of them', as they turned away to the darkness.

The snow-covered hedges, the low walls, the masses of the trees, the little paths turning to right and left, all brought a message and tried to speak to the two women and the child who walked among them, shining their lantern over them, awed by the presence of unseen things, the arch of stars above, their thoughts on God.

Susan's lips moved as she passed old friends, shrouded in white, yet intensely alive and quivering. When they reached the oak tree in the midst of the field up which they climbed, they stopped with one accord to rest.

'I was ready for my wind,' said Becky, puffing.

'Stars are grand tonight,' she continued. 'They are candles lit by God, and however He does it I don't know.'

They looked up to the light of the Milky Way, stretching across the vault of the sky, from hill to hill, from Wild Boar Head to the wood by Archer's Brow. The stars seemed alive, the air was full of movement as they twinkled, and threw a shooting star down to the earth.

Margaret picked out the constellations, a snake with pointed head, a chair, a jewelled crown. They lost stars and found them, they put their heads together to see the same one, and pointed and cried as if they watched a show of fireworks.

But their feet were cold and they turned their eyes to the

earth, and walked on up the hill towards the dark mass of buildings at the top.

'The teacher says they are other worlds,' said Susan.

'We shall all know in good time,' answered Margaret philosophically, 'worlds or angels' eyes, or visions of heaven,' and Susan decided the teacher was wrong, they were the guardian angels watching over the flocks and people who were out at night, and beyond were the golden streets and jasper walls of Heaven.

They passed under the giant beech trees, which stood very quiet with their burden of snow, by fields and hedges, to the orchard and the big gate. Roger barked and the doors flew open. They could see the square of light down the path, the radiance spread across the lawn and gilded the white laden trees.

They stamped the snow off their boots and removed the woollen coverings. Then they entered the warm fire-lit house, which looked like Aladdin's cave with its rows of shining brass candlesticks, its dish-covers, lustre jugs, guns, the warming-pan, and the gay decorations of holly, ivy, and flags.

The parlour table was laid for supper, Tom had been busy whilst they were away. There were mince pies, the green marbled cheese, and elderberry wine in the cut-glass decanter which had belonged to Tom's mother.

Afterwards Tom got out the concertina from its octagonal box and he dusted the tiny ivory keys and the flowered and berried sides with his silk handkerchief, gently, as if it were a child's face he was touching. Becky in great excitement gave out the hymn-books, for she dearly loved a bit of music, and she was to be invited into the room. He played his favourites of Moody and Sankey, with sweet trebles and droning basses, as they sang, in soft sad voices, tired yet happy. They knelt on the worn rose-covered carpet with their faces against the chairs, and said their prayers, putting their lives and their hopes, their seed-time and harvest, their cattle and crops in the hands of their Father.

CHAPTER 13

January

THE New Year hung in the air, hovering with wings outstretched above the farm, carrying joy and sorrow in its feathers, waiting, waiting for the big clock to strike twelve. Dan stood outside with his coat-collar up, shivering in the steely air, staring up at the sky and across the vast dark to the hills.

The New Year shook and swooped down as the clock began to strike. Dan opened the door and entered as the last stroke died away, and the year flew in, filling the house at once, from the empty attics to the dairy where the milk froze in the pans.

Susan sat up in bed listening to the rush of wings, Becky wished for a sweetheart, and Margaret said a prayer. All the bells began to ring, Mellow Church pealed out a chime of bells, and the lone bell of Brue-on-the-Water called softly, or faded to nothing through the woods.

Dan hurried out again to Oak Meadow Farm. He had promised for a shilling to bring in the New Year for them, and it waited up above the oak trees whilst he took his lantern across the fields and waded through the snowdrifts, for the path had entirely gone. Mrs Wolff's hair was grey as ashes and so was her husband's, and their daughter, Mary, was a fair woman. They had had so much ill-luck in the past through their own red-headed Sandy coming in first, they now sent for dark Dan.

A mug of ale and a pie waited for him, and he ate it as he stood in the low-raftered doorway, before he turned through the stretch of fields and lanes home again.

Susan had snuggled down in bed and fallen asleep, but

Margaret lay wondering what the year would bring forth. Tom was tired, he had a lot to do the next day, and he turned over and snored, but Margaret lay awake half the night wrestling with the angel of Fortune.

School began with snowballing and slides down the long roads. The big boys put stones inside their snowballs, which hurt, and poured water down the slides, so that the roads were like glass and all the little girls fell down, Susan came home, plunging through the snow in the wood, proud of the black rows of bruises on her legs. She took out her doll's wagon, a sturdy box with heavy wheels, which her father had made for her, and ran down a little cosy field by the house, perched on the top.

Then Tom made her a real toboggan, and she skimmed like a swallow on Saturday afternoon down the long hills under the blue shadows till dusk fell, and the rattle of cans on the wall told her milking was beginning.

She played alone, as always, but she shouted to the trees as she flew past them, and talked to the young moon in the sky as she dragged the sleigh up the long steep slopes.

Bright beams poured from the kitchen window, and fell over the hill up which she trudged, a little red-shantered figure, with a muffler round her neck and a brown coat wrapped round her body. Margaret came to the door and waved to the little speck she could see in the middle of the great white slope, and Susan came home with wet rosy cheeks and damp hair, snow sticking to her gloves and caked in ice over her back and side where she had fallen off when the sledge turned turtle.

From the oven came the smell of roast apples, the great brown teapot stood steaming on the table, and stacks of buttered toast, and enormous round tea-cakes piping hot, were piled on the plates.

'Roast apples and cream,' cried Susan, and she tore off her soaking boots and left them in their puddle on the sanded hearthstone.

Then Tom came in and joined them, with eyes sparkling

like the frosty stars, and later Becky came in, her hands chapped and red, her eyes bright, and hung her milking bonnet behind the servants' door. Dan ate his tea whilst Joshua and Becky harnessed Diamond and Tom got up to help them scye and measure the milk.

Then he returned to his tea, and Dan walked down the hill in plenty of time for the train, for the mare could only go slowly, and every minute he had to stop to clear her hoofs, and lead her through the dangerous parts. In his hand he carried a lantern to guide her feet through the drifts.

Those dark nights were detested by the farm hands, the wind was like a carving-knife and it cut their hands and cheeks till they bled. They wrapped mufflers round their necks when they crossed the fields, and Joshua wore mittens so that his fingers were free, but they were frozen like boards, and caked with ice.

But wall-mending, milking, cattle-feeding, and watering had to go on, the cow-houses and stables were cleaned, the hens, calves, pigs, and sheep had to be fed. Turnips must be chopped, and slices of dry clean hay cut as neatly from the stack as a slice of bread from the loaf, with no slattering or waste.

Tom cut the hay, for Dan was a slatterer and Joshua's head could not stand the height of the ladder, nor was his hand steady enough to hold the cutting-knife. So Tom cut and Dan trussed the hay and carried it to the barns ready for foddering, a walking haystack as he staggered across the snowy field with only his two legs showing.

But sometimes the snow was so deep that all work was stopped except the most essential, and Susan could no longer go to school with her little lantern through the fairy woods. That was bliss indeed, happiness for which she nightly prayed as she knelt by the bedroom fire.

Then they lived as remote and self-contained as the Swiss Family Robinson, on a white island, cut off from every-thing, the post, and the station news. For the milk had to be

kept at home, the mare could not get down the hill, through
the deep drifts, and Margaret and Becky made butter instead. In the dairy lay dishes of golden pats, round and oblong, with the corn-sheaves and cows imprinted upon them,
or criss-cross and diamonds. Butter was salted and stored in
brown crocks to preserve it.

Winter laid siege, but they were well garrisoned and pro-
visioned, with barn and larder full.

When the door was opened the walls, steps, and the dog-
kennel had disappeared, and against the door itself leaned a
great wall of snow. The windows were dark and a strange
silence spread over everything, filling the house and its dim
rooms.

Then Dan and Tom and Joshua shovelled their way to
the nearest barn and brought out spades and a barrow.
They dug out a path to each cow-house door, the stables,
the pig-cotes, the water-troughs, and various buildings. All
day they dug, making solid walls on either side of their paths,
silently shovelling, and all day the snow softly fell. Each day
they worked, feeding the stock, held up in everything except
the continual digging.

Susan was filled with the most intense happiness. It was
marvellous, this shut-off world, this whiteness and stillness.
She wondered joyfully if it would last for a month, as she
sprinkled crumbs on the doorsteps and walls.

But Tom was anxious about the sheep which were in the
fold across the fields, and Becky grumbled at the extra work
with a house full of men, stamping the snow on the floors,
and the butter-making to do, and her fingers stiff and
cramped.

The thick ice on the troughs had to be broken every day
to fill the kettles and to water the cattle.

Susan walked through the narrow paths with the high
snow walls to look at the fields with their hidden walls and
trees with branches sweeping the ground. She froze little
bottles of water to make a burst, she collected icicles to eat,
and built a snow man by the door. But her father waded

across the wild fields, falling and floundering to the buildings where the sheep and stirks waited for food.

It was a world of air like daggers, stabbing the thin
human skin, freezing the heart on that high hillside. Little
birds dropped numb, and Tom picked them up with his
gentle fingers and brought them into the house to see if there
was any life in them. Susan nursed them in a basket and let
them loose in the barn if they recovered. The great doors of
one barn were left open for birds to take shelter, and Joshua
chopped the wood with little wings fluttering and tiny eyes
of robin and tit watching him. They slept on the hooks and
beams of the walls, on the pile of forks and rakes, and ate the
grains of corn fallen from the bins.

> ' The north wind doth blow and we shall have snow,
> And what will the robin do then, poor thing?
> He will sit in the barn and keep himself warm,
> And hide his head under his wing, poor thing,'

sang Susan, who thought that every nursery rhyme ori-
ginated at Windystone.

Rain came and the whiteness became transparent, before
it disappeared in torrents which swept down the lanes. The
floods made the wild little river a spate, which rose over its
banks, and covered the roads so that the carts splashed
through with unwilling horses, shying at the flickering
lights.

Still the rain fell and Susan could not go to school. She
wondered if it was the coming of the end of the world. The
river would rise, higher and higher, covering Mellow and
Dangle, and joyfully drowning the school. At Windystone
they would be safe on their hill, no flood could ever rise so
high. The water would fill the valleys all round, and boats
would rescue the people from their bedrooms and the cattle
from their stalls. They would sail up the hills to the farm-
land which would poke out like an island with Noah's Ark
in the middle.

She stood at the window watching the rain pouring from

the leaden skies down the fields, and waiting for the flood to begin. A pigeon flew to shelter in the open cart shed, and Becky fed it with corn. It should be the dove she would send through her bedroom window, flying over the watery waste till it found a leaf, a holly leaf it must be, for there was nothing else.

But if the floods rose higher and the farm were covered they would go to the top of Arrow Hill, and stand waiting for death, cows and horses, pigs and sheep, rabbits and foxes, and people all squeezed on the top of the hill, watching the water mount to drown them. But that couldn't be, the rainbow was the sign.

The rain ceased at last and Tom sent for Abel Fern, the hedger and ditcher. He was a strong leather-faced man, with six or seven children, one of whom met him each night to help to carry the scraps Margaret had given him and the rabbits he had hidden in the hedges as he brashed. He worked with a sack thrown over his shoulders, tied round his neck with a piece of thatching twine, and his leggings and middle too were encased in sacks, so that he looked like an Ancient Briton as he slung his bill-hook over his shoulder.

He trimmed the hedges which ran round most of the fields and cut short the straggling wild rose and gorse in the lanes. He opened out the ditches which were filled with last year's leaves, and made channels and soughs so that the spring water would run clear into the stone troughs, and the water-logged, low-lying hollows would drain. He cleared the weed from the pond in Dewy Pasture, and cut new slits in the grass.

At night Margaret and Becky sat with the heavy rug across their knees, and a pile of strips on the floor, which they pegged in a design of reds and greys. Joshua cut spelds and Tom played little tunes on the concertina. Or they went into the parlour where the piano stood with frozen keys, and a fire burned unheeded most days, and listened while Susan played her hymns.

Every night Margaret read aloud for some hours, too,

Bleak House, The Old Curiosity Shop, and *East Lynne,* and this she continued throughout the winter, to Susan's terror and delight. She played some little game to herself, but her ears were listening, and her mother never suspected it interested her until she found her crying over the death of Little Willie. Then she was sent off to bed before the reading began.

The work of the year went on and the men were busy every day, manuring the mowing fields, chain-harrowing with the rippling steel harrow, and then rolling. Bonny drew the stone roller up and down the meadows for days, on the level patches where the crops were heavier.

One Saturday the shooters came, and Sir Harry Vane brought a party to lunch at Windystone. Early in the morning the beaters spread out into the woods, and the sound of firing came all the day to the farm. The men prepared forms and trestle tables in the cart-shed for the beaters' lunch. Later, smart yellow carts drove up with Sir Harry's crest on their sides, and footmen and cooks invaded the house.

They carried luncheon baskets to the kitchen and outer kitchen, and took out beautiful copper saucepans filled with savoury messes which they put on the stove. They unwrapped cheese, rich strange cheeses with foreign smells, and white crisp celery, brown rolls like balls, and bottles of wine in straw jackets. They had sirloins of beef and tongues, cold chickens and galantines, all white-frilled and fur-belowed, with silver skewers stabbing their middles.

They had rosy apples and golden pears, bunches of bloomy grapes, melons and nuts, just like the fruits in a fairy tale.

Susan sat like a mouse out of the way of the bustle, on the settle, watching the cook with his white cap and the footmen unpack the things. Mrs Garland and Becky set the big table with the extra leaf in the parlour, and a table in the south parlour for the guests. They got out the best damask cloths, and polished all the silver for the tables. They carried chairs from upstairs, quaint old bedroom chairs and ancient oak stools.

Then the party arrived, and the noise and excitement grew intense. Susan ran upstairs to look through the bedroom windows. On the green grassy bank were ranged rows of rabbits, all fastened in couples. Gamekeepers in cloth leggings, with black dogs snuffling round, put the pheasants in braces, the brilliant long-tailed male and his little brown wife, for Susan never doubted they knew which hen belonged to each cock, all still and dead.

But it was not sorrowful, it was wonderful and fine, the soft fur and bright peacock-coloured feathers, the smell of gunpowder, the pile of cartridge-cases, the crowd of men, the ladies in tweeds, the moving dogs, the beaters, old men and young thronging the yard, overflowing on the grass plot and lawn, jumping the low walls, walking in and out of stables and barns as if they lived there, yet with deference to her father who laughed and joked with everybody.

They recalled other shoots in past years, and recounted the scores of rabbits and the long lines of pheasants. Tom wondered what he would do with them all if he were Sir Harry. He would certainly give many to the farmers upon whose lands they fed.

Then the clatter of knives and forks began, and the sound of voices and laughter from the house. Susan ran downstairs to her corner again. The cook gave her a taste of the spicy jugged hare, and a slip of toast with minced chicken, a sugary mince pie, and a pear, a feast from Eve's Court.

Then the heavy smell of wines and cigars floated out, and the talk became louder. The door opened and the shooters went away. But while the smooth-voiced servants sat down in the kitchen for their meal, Susan, who was shy, escaped and went into the parlours. She sniffed in the wine-glasses and drank the dregs and tasted the broken rolls. She ran round like a dog in a strange room, with her nose poking into corners, enjoying the whiffs of blue smoke which stayed in the air. Bunches of grapes and some pears lay on the sideboard, but she knew better than to touch them, God was watching her.

Outside, the beaters had finished their bread and cheese in the cart-sheds, and were starting off with sticks in their hands to draw the next woods. The guns walked across the fields, and the bright chestnut horses were harnessed to the yellow carts. The hampers were repacked, but the fragments were left behind. The stews and half-cut chickens, the hares and pieces of beef, the celery and the exotic cheese all graced the Garlands' board, but the cheese ended in the mouse trap.

Sir Harry was fond of Farmer Garland and repaid him well for his trouble. He left two brace of pheasants, and pressed gold sovereigns in Margaret's hand. Even Becky and old Joshua had their golden bit.

The house dropped back to its old quiet, the clock ticking as if it had watched every movement, and enjoyed the stir and to-do as much as anybody.

After the mild interval the weather changed again, and wild days followed. The wind shrieked round the house, and howled at the door. Margaret read aloud a story of Canadian wolves which was more suitable to Susan than *East Lynne*, and Susan was petrified with fear, but dare not say anything lest the story should stop.

She could hear them snuffling outside the door, and when her father unlatched it to go out, and the wind snarled and flung it out of his hand, she sprang up expecting a pack of gaunt, fierce-eyed wolves would fill the house and devour them all. It required all her courage to go into the hall and walk across through the shadows, upstairs with the tiny light of the flickering candle which blew out as often as not and left her cut off from the bright, happy room, alone with the wolves who might have slipped in unseen.

An oak tree on one of the hills crashed down in the night, and a branch of a sycamore across the grass-plot fell. Little boughs were smashed off the apple trees, and one tree was uprooted. The pear tree was half torn from the side of the house, and piles of timber were blown down. But the house and farm were safe, never a tile was moved or a chimney touched, for it had weathered fiercer gales than this, when even men had been blown over and no one could go out except to crawl close to the ground.

The wood was strewn with branches as Susan battled her way through. The trees creaked and groaned so loudly they drowned the roar of the wind. She was swept from her path, flung against one tree, butted into another, slapped, smacked, and buffeted, but she fought doggedly on. When the wind was behind her she felt she could sit on it, and be carried along like a happy feather. She skimmed over the road, pretending to fly.

At night she could not light her lantern, and she was scratched and bruised as she panted along in the dark, falling over the broken boughs which lay in her path, swept by dipping boughs, with raging packs of wolves hot on her track, before she reached the blessed haven of the house.

'Let us pray for the poor folk without a home tonight,' said Margaret, and they knelt down round the fire before Susan went upstairs to her bedroom.

CHAPTER 14

The Easter Egg

ONE morning Susan looked out of her window and saw that spring had really come. She could smell it and she put her head far out, until she could touch the budding elm twigs. She pressed her hands on the rough stone of the window-sill to keep herself from falling as she took in deep draughts of the wine-filled air.

It was the elder; the sap was rushing up the pithy stems, the young leaves had pierced the buds, and now stuck out like green ears listening to the sounds of spring. The rich heady smell from the pale speckled branches came in waves, borne by soft winds, mixed with the pungent odour of young nettles and dock.

She wrinkled her nose with pleasure and a rabbit with her little one directly below the window, on the steep slope, wrinkled her nose, too, as she sat up among the nettles and borage.

Miss Susanna Dickory, Susan's godmother, had stayed at the farm a fortnight, and now Susan felt lost without her. It had been a time of delight to meet lavender in pockets of air on the stairs. Such delicious smells hovered about the house, such rustlings of silken skirts, and yap-yaps of the little be-ribboned, long-haired dog, Twinkle, as unlike Roger as a toy boat is unlike a man-o'-war.

'Twinkle, Twinkle, Twinkle,' she called in her high silvery voice, which made Dan laugh up his sleeve. It was for all the world like the harness bells, he told Becky.

She had come to visit her dear friend, Margaret, and to see her little god-child, Susan, and if she was disappointed in the child and found her a shy young colt, she said nothing.

She was a frail old lady, delicate-looking and fastidious, but she walked in the cow-sheds and sat down in the barns with her silk petticoats trailing in the dust, so that Joshua ran for the besom to sweep before her, and he actually took off his coat for her to step upon, like Sir Walter Raleigh, but Miss Dickory wouldn't.

Every day the Garlands had dinner and tea in the parlour, and every day the Worcester china was used. Becky put on a clean white cap and apron, and Dan brushed his coat and changed his collar, and scrubbed all the manure off his boots before he sat down in the kitchen, lest she should come in.

She slept in the big four-poster in the parlour bedroom and wore a lace night-cap, for Susan saw it when Becky took up her breakfast on a tray. Twinkle slept in a basket lined with silk at the foot of her bed. It was all most astonishing, like being in church all the time, and Christmas every day.

But now she had gone and only a few little corners of sweet smells remained. Susan sighed as she thought of her, and laughed at the rabbit, and then ran downstairs. It was Good Friday and she had a holiday for a week.

Her mother met her in the hall, running excitedly to call her. There was a parcel addressed to Mr, Mrs, and Miss Garland. Susan had never been called Miss before, except by the old man at the village who said, 'You're late, Missie,' when she ran past his cottage on the way to school.

With trembling fingers Susan and Margaret untied the knots, for never, never had anyone at Windystone been so wasteful as to cut a piece of string.

Inside was a flower-embroidered table-cloth for Margaret, a book of the Christian Saints and Martyrs of the Church for Tom, which he took with wondering eyes, and a box containing six Easter eggs.

There were three chocolate eggs, covered with silver paper, a wooden egg painted with pictures round the edge, a red egg with a snake inside, and a beautiful pale blue velvet egg lined with golden starry paper. It was a dream.

Never before had Susan seen anything so lovely. Only once had she ever seen an Easter egg (for such luxuries were not to be found in the shops at Broomy Vale), and then it had been associated with her disgrace.

Last Easter Mrs Garland had called at the vicarage with her missionary box and taken Susan with her. Mrs Stone had asked Margaret to make some shirts for the heathen, and whilst they had gone in the sewing-room to look at the pattern, Susan, who had been sitting silent and shy on the edge of her chair, was left alone.

The room chattered to her; she sprang up, wide-awake, and stared round. She had learnt quite a lot about the habits of the family from the table and chairs, when her eye unfortunately spied a fat chocolate egg, a bloated enormous egg, on a desk before the window. Round its stomach was tied a blue ribbon, like a sash.

Susan gazed in astonishment. What was it for? She put out a finger and stroked its glossy surface. Then she gave it a tiny press of encouragement, and, oh! her finger went through and left a little hole. The egg must have been soft with the sunshine. But who would have thought it was hollow, a sham?

She ran and sat down again, deliberating whether to say something at once or to wait till she was alone with her mother. Mrs Stone returned with Margaret saying, 'Yes, Mrs Stone, of course I won't forget the gussets. The heathen jump about a good deal, they will need plenty of room.' But before Susan could speak, a long-haired, beaky-nosed girl ran into the room, stared at Susan and went straight to the Easter egg.

'Who's been touching *my* Easter egg?' she cried, just like the three bears.

They all looked at Susan and with deep blushes she whispered, 'I did.'

They all talked at once, Margaret was full of apologies and shame, Mrs Stone said it didn't matter, but of course you could see it did, and the bear rumbled and growled.

When she got home Susan had to kneel down at once and say a prayer of forgiveness, although it was the middle of the morning. 'You know, Susan, it's very wrong to touch what isn't yours.'

But this perfect blue egg! There was never one like it. She put it in her little drawer in the table where her treasures were kept, the book of pressed flowers, the book of texts in the shape of a bunch of violets, the velvet Christmas card with the silk fringe, and the card that came this Christmas.

Tenderly she touched them all. In the egg she placed her ring with the red stone, and a drop of quicksilver which had come from the barometer. She closed the drawer and went off to tell anyone who would listen, the trees, Dan, the clock, Roger, Duchess, or Fanny.

But what a tale to tell the girls at school! She wouldn't take it there or it might get hurt, a rough boy might snatch it from her, or the teacher might see her with it and put it in her desk.

'Mother, may I ask someone to tea to see my egg?' she asked, fearing in her heart that no one would come so far.

'Yes, my dear,' and Margaret smiled at her enthusiasm, 'ask whoever you like.'

She hurried through the woods and along the lanes to school, saying to herself, 'Do you know what I had at Easter? No. Guess what I had at Easter. No. My godmother, who is a real lady, sent me such a lovely Easter present. It was a box of eggs, and one was made of sky-blue velvet and lined with golden stars.'

She was late and had to run, and when she passed the little cottage with the brass door-knocker and a canary in the window, the nice old man with a beard said, 'You are going to be late this morning, Missie,' as he looked at his turnip watch. It was very kind of him, and Susan thanked him politely before she took to her heels.

She toiled up the hill, a stitch in her side, and her face wet with perspiration, past the cottages with babies at the open doors and cats by the fire, past the silent gabled house where two old ladies lived, and the old cottage where the witch pottered about, and the lovely farm where she some-times went to tea with her mother, and sat very still listening to the ancient man who lived there.

The bell stopped ringing and she was late. She would be caned, she had no excuse. She heard the Lord's Prayer and the hymn as she took off her hat and cape, and hung them on the hook. She listened to the high voices and watched the door handle, waiting to slip in at the sound of Amen. Her little red tongue glided over the palm of her hand, to pre-pare for the inevitable. There was a shuffle of feet and she turned the knob. All eyes switched her way as she walked up to the desk.

'Any excuse, Susan Garland?'

She dumbly held out her hand. Down came the cane three times on the soft flesh. Biting her lip and keeping back her tears she walked to her place, and bound her handker-chief round the hot stinging palm. Yes, there were three marks, three red stripes across it.

Curious eyes watched her to see if she would cry, and she smiled round and whispered, 'It didn't hurt a bit', but her hand throbbed under her pinafore, and the fingers curled protectingly round it as if they were sorry. It was an honour to be caned and to bear the strokes unflinchingly. Susan showed her marks to the girls round her, and then whispered, 'I've got a blue velvet egg. Tell you about it at playtime.'

At break the children walked orderly to the door and then flung themselves out into the playground, to jump and 'twizzle', hop and skip, to dig in their gardens, or play hide-and-seek.

Susan had a circle of girls round her looking at the weals and listening to the tale of the egg. They strolled under the chestnut trees with their arms round each other.

'It's blue velvet, sky-blue, and inside it is lined with paper covered with gold stars. It's the most beautiful egg I ever saw.' The girls opened their eyes and shook their curls in amazement.

'Bring it to school for us to see,' said Anne Frost, her friend.

'I daren't, Mother wouldn't let me, but you can come to tea and see it.'

'Can I?' asked one. 'Can I?' asked another.

Susan felt like a queen and invited them all. Big girls came to her, and she invited them. The rumour spread that Susan Garland was having a lot of girls to tea. Tiny little girls ran up and she said they might come too. She didn't know where to draw the line, and in the end the whole school of girls invited themselves.

They ran home to Dangle and Raddle at dinner-time to say that Susan Garland was having a party, and they were brushed and washed and put into clean pinafores and frocks, with blue necklaces and Sunday hair-ribbons.

Susan sat on a low stone wall eating her sandwiches, excited and happy. She was sure they would all be welcome and she looked forward to the company in the Dark Wood.

After school she started off with a crowd of fifty girls, holding each other's hands, arms entwined round Susan's waist, all pressed up close to her. They filled the narrow road like a migration, or the Israelites leaving the bondage of Egypt.

Mothers came to their doors to see them pass, and waved their hands to their little daughters. 'Those Garlands must have plenty of money,' said they.

Susan was filled with pride to show her beautiful home, the fields and buildings, the haystacks, the bull, and her kind mother and father, and Becky and Joshua who would receive them.

They went noisily through the wood, chattering and gay, astonished at the long journey and the darkness of the trees, clinging to one another on the little path lest an adder or fox should come out, giggling and pushing each other into the leaves. The squirrels looked down in wonder, and all ghostly things fled.

Margaret happened to stand on the bank that day to

watch for Susan's appearance at the end of the wood; she always felt slightly anxious if the child were late.

She could scarcely believe her eyes. There was Susan in her grey cape and the new scarlet tam-o'-shanter, but with her came a swarm of children. She had forgotten all about the vague invitation.

Was the child bringing the whole school home?

She ran back to the house and called Becky and Joshua. They stood dumbfounded, looking across the fields.

'We shall have to give them all something to eat, coming all that way,' she groaned.

'It will be like feeding the five thousand in the Bible,' exclaimed Becky, and Joshua stood gaping. He had never known such a thing. What had come over the little maid to ask such a rabble?

They went to the kitchen and dairy to take stock. There was Becky's new batch of bread, the great earthenware crock full to the brim, standing on the larder floor. There was a dish of butter ready for the shops, and baskets of eggs counted out, eighteen a shilling. There was a tin of brandy snaps, to last for months, some enormous jam pasties, besides three plum cakes.

They set to work, cutting and spreading on the big table, filling bread and butter plates with thick slices.

Joshua filled the copper kettles and put them on the fire, and counted out four dozen eggs, which he put on to boil. 'We can boil more when we've counted the lasses.'

Roger nearly went crazy when he saw the tribe come straggling and tired up the path to the front of the house. Susan left them resting on the wall and went in to her mother.

'I've brought some girls to tea, Mother,' she said, opening her eyes at the preparations.

'Oh, indeed,' said Mrs Garland. 'How many have you brought?'

'A lot,' answered Susan. 'Where's my egg, they want to see it?'

'Susan Garland,' said Margaret severely, taking her by the shoulders, 'whatever do you mean by bringing all those girls home with you? Don't talk about that egg. Don't you see that they must all be fed? We can't let them come all this way without a good tea. You mustn't think of the egg, you will have to work.'

Susan looked aghast, she realized what she had done and began to cry.

'Never mind, dry your eyes at once and smile. I don't know what your father will say, but we will try to get them fed before he comes.'

Margaret began to enjoy herself, she was a born hostess and here was a chance to exercise her hospitality.

She went out to the children and invited them to have a wash at the back door, where she had put a pancheon of hot water and towels. Then they were to sit orderly on the low walls, along the front of the house, and wait for tea which would come out in a few minutes. She chose four girls to help to carry the things, and then she returned, leaving smiles and anticipation.

The fifty trooped round the house and washed their hands and faces, with laughter and glee. They peeped at the troughs, and admired the pig-cotes, but Susan shepherded them back to the walls where they sat in their white pinafores like swallows ready for flight.

Becky and Joshua carried out the great copper tea-urn, which was used at farm suppers and sometimes lent for church parties. Margaret collected every cup and mug, basin and bowl in the house, from the capacious kitchen cupboards and tall-boy, the parlour cupboards, the shelves, the dressers, from corner cupboards upstairs, from china cabinet stand, and what-not, from brackets and pedestals.

There were Jubilee mugs, and gold lustre mugs, an old china mug with 'Susan Garland, 1840', on it, and several with 'A present for a Good Girl'. There were mugs with views and mugs with wreaths of pink and blue flowers, with mottoes and proverbs, with old men in high hats and women in wide skirts. There were tin mugs which belonged to the Irishmen, and Sheffield plated mugs from the mantelpiece, pewter and earthenware. There were delicate cups of lovely china, decorated with flowers and birds, blue Wedgwood, and some Spode breakfast cups, besides little basins and fluted bowls.

Margaret gave out the cups and mugs herself, choosing clean, careful-looking girls for her best china. The social position of each girl could be detected at once from the kind of cup she had, which was unlike Margaret's usual procedure, but this was an exceptional occasion. If only they had been round a table she would have trusted them, but now she had to use her judgement.

Becky poured out the tea, and Susan took it to each girl, with new milk and brown sugar. Old Joshua, wearing an apron, walked along the rows with a clothes-basket of bread and butter and a basket of eggs. As soon as he got to the end he began again.

Margaret took over the tea, and sent Becky to cut more and more. Susan's legs ached and an immense hunger seized

her, she had eaten nothing but sandwiches since her breakfast at half past seven. But there was no time, the girls
clamoured for more, and she ran backwards and forwards
with her four helpers, who had their own tea in between.

A clothes-basket was filled with cut-up pieces of cake,
pastry, slabs of the men's cake, apple pasty, and currant
slices. Then the box of ginger-snaps was taken round, and
some girls actually refused. The end was approaching, but
still Joshua walked up and down the line with food.

Dan came from out of the cow-houses with the milk, and
Tom followed. Nobody had been in the smaller cow-houses.
What was Joshua doing in an apron, and Becky too when
she should be milking?

He stared at the rows of chattering children and walked
in the house. Margaret ran in to explain.

'Don't be cross with her,' she said.

He said nothing till Susan came in for more cake.

Then he stood up and looked at her, and Susan quailed.

'Dang my buttons, Susan Garland, if you are not the most
silly soft lass I ever knew! Are you clean daft crazy to bring
all that crowd of cackling childer here?'

Then he stamped out to the byres and Susan walked back
with her slices of cake, thankful she had not been sent to bed.

At last the feast was finished and Becky and Margaret
washed up the cups and mugs, and collected the egg-shells,
whilst Joshua went milking and Susan ran for a ball to give
them a game in the field before they went home. They ran
races and played hide-and-seek, and lerky, they played
ticky-ticky-touch-stone round the great menhir, and
swarmed over its surface.

At the end of an hour Margaret rang a bell and they came
racing to her. 'Put on your coats now, my dears, and go
home, your mothers will expect you, and you have a long
walk before you.'

So they said goodbye, and ran off singing and happy,
down the hill. Two little girls had come shyly up to Susan
with a parcel before they went.

'Mother said if it was your birthday we were to give you this,' and they held out a ball like a pineapple. But Susan had to confess it wasn't her birthday and they took it home.

She went indoors and sat down, tired and famished, at the table. 'And, Mother, I never showed them my sky-blue egg after all! But they did enjoy themselves.'

CHAPTER 15

Spring

Soon the plum blossom came out on the knotted black tree which climbed all over the Irishmen's Place, at the gable of one of the buildings, covering the long window slits with a network of close branches. A chaffinch built her nest in a crook in its boughs. Cream petals came thick among the pointed leaves of the pear trees, and a little brown bird lived right in the midst of the fragrance. Susan could put her head out of her mother's window and peep at the bright eyes among the leaves.

The double white lilac at the garden gate and the purple and lavender bushes hanging over the pig-cotes budded, and the lovely soft apple-green leaves burst through the javelin points. Starlings built in the hole in the giant apple tree which overshadowed the lawn and horse-trough, the ancient tree taller than Windystone itself, perhaps older, hollow as a skull, yet soon to be covered with blossom and little green fruit.

Doves cooed in the larch plantation, under the blue-speckled sky, jays screamed in the spinney and flashed their wings defiantly at the stealthy gamekeepers.

Magnificent pheasants rang out their challenge as they flew boldly clattering over the garden to the Druid Wood. Squirrels ran up and down the mossy walls and chased each other up the nut trees by the cow-sheds. A yellow stoat crept warily over the wall by the yew trees and rats slunk in the shadows of the stack-yard towards a hen-coop. The cock crew with a shrill note and the hen clucked to her chicks and cried fiercely, with flapping wings. The shadow of a hawk went over the young chickens, death in the blue sky, and every chick ran obediently to its mother, except one tiny stray upon which the savage claws and beak swooped.

Tom Garland ran out with his double-barrelled gun many a time a day, for it was Nature's birth time, and the little creatures were in danger from their enemies. The men had been busy since early in the year with the sheep, and now the lambs were merry curly-haired little rogues, with twinkling eyes and black sturdy legs.

They spent their baby days in Whitewell field, near the house, cropping a few morsels of short sweet grass, nuzzling and suckling from their mothers, and playing like school-children.

A lamb ran calling plaintively after a sheep, but she walked on, eating steadily, heartless, as he tried to push under her. He stood, puzzled, his first disillusion, and then, bleating and crying, he found his own true mother. With tail wagging and little firmly planted legs, he drank until the impatient mother gave him a push and sent him off to play. He stared round and then galloped to the others who were in the midst of a game.

Every year, for two hundred years at least, lambs ran the same race in Whitewell field. In other fields they had their odd games, but here it was always the same.

By the side of one of the paths stood the oak tree, with the seat under it, and a short distance away stood the great spreading ash. The lambs formed up in a line at the oak, and at some signal they raced to the ash, as fast as their tiny legs would go; then they wheeled round and tore back again. They held a little talk, a consultation, nose-rubbing, friendly pushes, and then off they went again on their race-track.

On the first of May the cows left their winter quarters in the cow-houses, and were turned out to graze in the fields. That was a day to remember. Becky put her hands on her hips and shouted with laughter at their antics as they came push-ing, tumbling through the gate and galloped wildly up and down the hills, with outstretching tails and tossing horns. They flung their heads back and blorted, they stamped their feet on the cool soft earth, they leapt like young lambs and danced with their unwieldy bodies on their slender legs.

Cows that had long been jealous attacked each other with curved horns, and the farmer and Dan stood ready with forks and sticks to prevent any harm. They raised their noses in the air and sniffed the smells of spring, and they ran to the streams and water-troughs, trampling the clear fresh water, drinking deeply with noisy gulps. They explored their old haunts, rubbed their flanks against their favourite stumps and railings, scratched their heads, polished their horns, and then settled down to eat the young short sweet grass.

The bull in the byre stamped and roared to be free with them, but he was dangerous, his horns were short and deep, and his eyes red. No man turned his back on him, but Tom never let him think he was master. They had had some tussles and he obeyed the farmer, but old Joshua kept away from him.

There were deaths as well as births on the farm, losses as well as gains. One day a man was seen waving and shouting as he came running across the Alder Lease. Tom stood at the back door, looking down the hill at the meadows below, straining to hear what he said. It was the servant from Oak Meadows and he pointed as he ran to a hollow by a wall out of sight. When he got near enough the words floated up the hill, 'A cow fallen in the ditch yonder.'

'Get the ropes, quick,' cried Tom, with fear in his voice, and he and Dan ran down the fields with the heavy ropes and Joshua followed with a spade. Becky went too, to give a hand in pulling the poor beast, and Margaret stood pale and anxious at the door.

There it lay on its back where it had slipped in the wet treacherous grass, as it tried to get the bright patch across the little ditch. A child could have scrambled out, but the cow's legs were twisted, and it moaned very softly.

They put the ropes round it and hauled, but the sloping

field and sudden drop made it difficult, the five of them could not move it. It lay with agonized eyes, imploring help. Its leg was broken, perhaps its back was injured, and above was the blue sky and larks singing.

'Get the gun and a cartridge,' muttered Tom, and Becky hurried up the steep hills and across the fields. But it was too late, it was dead, and there it lay, a great white lump, smeared with mud and grass. They walked up the hill a sad procession, weary, disheartened. Margaret met them, troubled.

The next day a knacker took it away, some silver for the skin, that was all. It went down the hill with its legs sticking out, tragic and unreal, and an empty stall had to be filled.

Then someone, one of those folk who walk up and down the hills staring at nothing and asking foolish questions, left the gates open. Duchess's foal, a chestnut with a star, glossy as the nut itself, got out and ran in his young innocence to the new horse who was a kicker. He let fly, and Prince was lamed, spoilt.

They had the vet, and his leg was rubbed and fomented, but he would always limp. Tom grew grave and worked harder than ever. Susan's heart burst with sorrow, but between herself and the grown-ups existed a barrier she could never cross.

Days grew longer and the mists of dawn were swept away by the sun growing stronger. Heavy scents of the earth itself filled the air as the plough turned up the deep brown soil. Duchess and Diamond walked up and down the ploughland, and Dan guided them in the hollows and low hills as he drew the straight lines on the earth. Thrushes sang on the sycamore trees which stood round the walls of the plough-land, with long, pink, swelling buds.

Primroses made pale pools of light under the hedges, and along the steep banks, where they grew in spite of winds which suddenly swept up the valleys and over the hills with a fierceness which tore the blossom from the pear trees. But the flowers on the banks were small, short-stalked little ones, whilst those under last year's leaves in the hedgerows were large and fine.

Margaret, Becky, and Susan went off to the fields to pick cowslips, for the time had come to make cowslip wine. It was a cowslip day, too, a day of scents and pale gold colours, of glittering budded trees and little winds which clasped their skirts and tickled their ankles. The sky was fair, soft, yellow as a cowslip ball, and clouds like butterflies flew across it.

They each took a small basket, and Becky and Margaret carried two clothes-baskets between them. They left these under a tree on the side of the hill whilst they gathered the most fragrant and elusive of all field flowers.

Cowslips have whims and fancies on the hillsides. They love and they detest, they pick and choose their dwelling-place. They do not come up year after year in a wealth of yellow, like their neighbours the primroses, whose buds Susan knew would always lie in their nest of deeply veined green leaves among last year's oak and beech under the hedges. They grow in clusters in family groups on the exposed hills, moving and migrating, a patch here one year, and gone the next to a sunnier spot.

Some years they sprinkle the meadows with heavy gold, and at other times they hardly come up, their flowers are small and reluctant, as if they wish just to peep out, and then return to the warm earth.

But this was a good year, and Becky and Mrs Garland picked rapidly, filling their baskets and pouring the yellow flood into the clothes-baskets. Susan worked slowly, whispering to the flowers, searching for larger and larger ones, condoling with little ones, and leaving two together lest one should be lonely.

She snapped the crisp stalks and sucked many a tiny scarlet-spotted floret to get the honey from the bottom, like a bee, which she resembled in her brown frock as she crouched on the grass. Now and then she found an oxlip, a

king among the cowslips, and then she held it up to the sky,
shut her eyes, and wished:

> *'I wish for a pony all my own.*
> *I wish for curly hair.*
> *I wish to see a fairy.'*

Oxlips share with falling stars, the new moon, white bluebells, the first cuckoo, and four-leaved clover the property of
granting a wish.

'Do get on, Susan,' called Margaret, pausing for a moment to rest her back and to look at the child with her face
uplifted. 'Your basket isn't half filled.'

'I was wishing, Mother. I found a family of oxlips.'

'Work comes before wishing. "If wishes were horses
beggars would ride",' returned her mother, and she bent
once more to the task. But Susan saw a troop of tiny beggars
with green rags floating from their arms, riding through the
meadows on the oxlips' backs, whipping their steeds with
chimney-sweepers whilst the oxlips tossed their heads, and
champed at their bits and rang their bells.

The cocks crowed, one against another, and the hens ran
to meet Tom Garland as he crossed the field. They trotted
behind him, red, white, and speckled, their little feet scutter-
ing, their heads strained forward in expectant haste, jostling,
pushing, like the rats after the Pied Piper. He waved his
hand to the cowslip-pickers in the next field, and disappeared in the barn. The hens and cocks waited outside,
cackling to one another.

He leaned over the half-door, and sent a golden rain of
Indian corn over them. More hens came fluttering, screaming, and screeching under the gates, through the hen-gap in
the wall, and running down the narrow stairs from their
house, lest they should be too late.

The workers returned for dinner, and then went off to the
fields again. Susan was tired, but her help was needed. All
day they picked, and Dan joined them for an hour until the
baskets were full. They carried them home at milking-time,

piled heaps of scented blossoms and Susan ran in front, singing and shouting, her tiredness all gone.

She opened the gates and closed them carefully after the baskets had passed. She called to the echo, 'Cowslip wine', and the echo answered. She startled the rabbits which sat up under the walls with little praying paws uplifted, wondering at the unusual noise in the quiet fields. She led the mare by

the forelock from the farm gate, where it stood waiting to be invited within to the warmth.

The kitchen fire was low and the house looked dark after the light of the fields. Becky fetched sticks from the barn, and soon the flames roared up the chimney. Susan took the big copper kettle to the troughs, where the ferns were unfolding their brown fists. She dipped the lading-can into the water until the kettle brimmed over on the ground and the water ran through the wall down the cliff. Then Becky carried it in and lifted it on the stove.

Margaret sliced some cheese and put it in the Dutch oven and Becky went off to help with the milk. Soon the milkers came home with their cans for cooling, measuring, and scying.

But after tea they placed the clothes-baskets on the hearthrug and drew up their chairs, to finish the cowslips.

They picked off the 'peeps' and dropped them into an immense earthenware crock, but the green stalks and sheaths were thrown on the floor.

Tom Garland sat outside on the stone bench whilst all the 'peeping' went on, and looked over the valley below, where his fields dipped down to the river, and then climbed up to the rocky slopes above. Even at that time the vivid mowing-fields could be distinguished from the pasture-land, which was dull green, all hills and hollows, with springs and woods breaking its colour.

Masses of black lichened stones like crouching elephants broke through the earth, and sheep lay close under their shelter, and rough-coated stirks pressed against them.

All round the violet dusk was creeping, and a mist already lay in the bottom fields, hiding the bushes and hedges in its soft white cloak.

Then solitary lights shone from farms far away, and one on the highest spur of a distant hill twinkled like a star.

'Noah Peace has one of those new lamps, I reckon, it shines as bright as the full moon,' called Tom to his wife through the open doors and passage. His voice was low, in keeping with the quiet of the hillsides. He stared at the light, pondering, dreaming, wrapt in the creeping dusk. Inside the house was the happy murmur of voices, but the sounds of night were sad.

An owl called anxiously to his mate and an answering mournful cry came from the orchard. A little bird ruffled the yew trees and the leaves rustled drily. Molly, the Jersey cow, mooed sadly in the cow-house, calling the calf which had been taken from her. A rabbit screamed like a child in the beech wood deep below the house, and Tom turned from the light on the hillside to stare through the dusky trees. A late blackbird cried 'Tchink, tchink' as it heard the hidden danger. In the Greeny Croft a horse cropped regularly and raised its head to snort. Far away a dog barked, so far that it seemed to be on another planet, a ghost dog.

Margaret left the cowslips and trimmed the lamp in the

half-dark. She hung it from the hook above the table and lighted it with a speld from the new-cut bundle on the shelf.

A new star now shone across the valleys, through the trees with their delicate lace-work, to the hills. Somebody far away said, 'Garlands have just lighted their lamp,' and shadowy people looked from their windows to this spur on the great hill, the only light in all the rolling darkness.

Moths dashed against the window with tiny thuds, and Margaret cried, 'Come in, Tom, the night air is bad for you.'

Tom slowly raised himself and closed the outside shutters. Margaret cottered them and tapped to see they were fast. Then he shut the door and left the fields to their sleep.

Susan was sent to bed, and Becky took her candle to fasten the remaining shutters.

The pile of peeps was growing high, and on the floor lay a mountain of pale green cowslips, robbed of their beauty and sweetness.

The biggest copper preserving-pan was lifted down by Dan and Tom, from its shelf, where it gleamed across a broad corner over the settle. Margaret made a syrup in it over the fire and Becky measured the peeps with the wooden measure, pouring them into yellow pancheons from the dairy. They both ladled the hot liquid over the flowers and took them to the stone benches to cool.

The next day Margaret added some brewer's yeast which Dan had brought up fresh from the village when he went with the milk, and stirred it with the big wooden spoon. In the cool morning, in the sunny afternoon, and at night when candles were lit she stirred the bowls, whirling the little flowers round and round in the scented liquor. For nine days the pancheons stood there, stirred every day by someone, visited every night and morning by Susan. The little withered flowers lay bunched together floating on the surface, the liquor was dull and lifeless.

Then Margaret strained it through muslin and poured it into a barrel with a quart of brandy. There it stood, bunged

up, catching the cobwebs and dust in the stone chamber,
waiting till it was ready to be bottled. It would change to a
sparkling yellow wine, and Margaret would give little fluted
glasses of it with a biscuit to morning visitors, the curate for
subscriptions, Sir Harry when he came for a chat with Tom,
an occasional dealer. It was more precious than elderberry
wine, which was the drink for cold weather, for snow and
sleet.

CHAPTER 16

The Three Chambers

EVERY day was more beautiful than the last. The banks
and hedgerows were blue with bird's-eye and ground ivy,
and the sun bloomed in the sky like a great shining rose in
a blue garden. Clouds like white unicorns, elephants, castles,
and dragons moved across the heavens from the Druid
Wood to the far-away beech plumes where they disappeared
in the far-away world. Little winds came twinkling down
the distances, ruffling the tree-tops, until they too ran away
to the big towns where they would be lost in dirty streets,
striving in vain to get back to their own leafy homes.

Sweet smells came from the woods, of young bracken and
moss, and the gum of the tasselled larch trees. In the hedges
the wild cherry with filmy blossom raked the sky as if it
sought for wisps of cloud to hang with its flowers. The first
bluebells were out, the short-stemmed tiny ones which
grew among the grass, always a little higher than the blades.
In the woods soon the great sheet of blue would spread like a
lake reflecting the sky, bluebells with long juicy stalks, snapping with a click as you picked them, leaving a thread of heavy
juice on fingers and thumb. But the small flowers had their
day first, the black chimney-sweepers, the yellow mountain
pansies which fluttered in the short soft grass of the highest
pastures, among the gorse and rocks, and the blue bird's-eye.

All day long something nid-nodded at the casement windows, climbing up the broad stone mullions, tapping at the
glass, like a robin who wanted to come in. Sprays of budding tea roses, gold and cream with deep red leaves, soon
to hang creamy-petalled and heavy with scent, but now
tightly closed, knocked at the bedrooms and peered in at

the stone room. Young green honeysuckle flapped its streamers against the landing windows, and another bush swayed round a gable of the house. Scarlet japonicas, which Susan must never, never touch, clasped the mullions of the parlour and kitchen. Shoots of pear and plum pushed against the old rooms, the apple chamber, the cheese chamber, precious blossom which would bring bad luck if you so much as picked a petal.

But the elm tree rapped at the attic windows, Tom's giant 'ellum', the friend of his childhood, which threw its shadow endearingly over the house and poured the soft delicate bunches of green pennies down the chimneys and through many an open window. Little discs of light and shade danced across the lawn, and ran in and out of the damson trees and lilac, flickering on the water-troughs, and stone paths, as the trees swayed up and down.

On a branch of box which encircled a flower bed perched a wren singing so sweet a song, so short a trill of pure music that Susan would not have been surprised if she had seen a wee man in a green coat fluting on a pipe. She watched its tiny throat throb as it gazed back into her eyes, unflinching and brave. Cock Robin could not be far away from his wife, Jenny Wren.

There he was, hopping up and down on the wall, waiting for her to move, stamping his feet on the brown club-moss, dipping in the shade of the grass and stone-crop.

Becky came out, carrying a tin full of bread soaked in water, and the robin fluttered near. 'The bold little madam,' she cried, ignoring his sex, 'there you are,' and she threw a piece on the grass.

Susan ran up. 'Are you going to the three chambers, Becky? Can I come with you? Do let me.'

Together they went down the flagged path, past the yew trees, along the grassy square, past the pig-cotes and their little garden, past the bleaching ground, to the stack-yard. They climbed up the steep outer steps over the big cow-house, with ferns filling every corner and cranny, higher and higher, till they reached the stone platform at the top. They stopped to rest and look over the half-cut stacks to the young larch trees, pale green and silver, and the immense beech wood which stretched before them. Great white clouds rolled across the sky. 'Blown by God's breath,' said Becky, and Susan saw God with puffed-out cheeks leaning down from heaven and blowing as she blew a dandelion clock.

A steep field rose in front of them, a rounded, curving field, with the contours of a baby giant, which climbed up to the beech wood and disappeared in a mist of forget-me-nots and bluebells under the wall at the top. Its little smooth hills hid mushrooms and puff-balls, rabbit holes and fairy rings.

Its grass was short and fine, it had always been a pasture, for no one could mow its hills and valleys, but it was scored by a thousand little footpaths, the smallest paths for field mice, tiny tracks for rabbits whose burrows shone red, and larger paths which curved regularly round the sides of the hillocks for sheep. The paths criss-crossed in a maze, a regular town of streets.

Across the upper part, under the beech wood, went an old Roman road, which travelled up the fields and over the crest to a village where some remains had been dug up from the gardens, an altar stone, a broken lamp, a little figure of a heathen god. Two centuries before it was the pack road used by travellers between the remote high villages, but now it was an unknown grassy lane bordered by briars and gorse, by mountain ash trees and broken rocks.

Near the bottom of the field was the cow road, which led through several of the fields, along which the cattle wandered to the pastures, and the hay carts crept in the heat of summer with their unsteady loads.

In every field there was a water-trough, for springs and underground streams were plentiful, in this field was a different water supply. The trough was deeply sunk in the ground, with rocks round it and boggy land below, where the water drained, but the water was orange-coloured, tasting strongly of iron, always cold, always fresh and never running dry. The little plants which covered the bottom were orange too, and one could bring up a handful of tawny gold slime, soft as velvet, which dried on the grass like rust. Susan went there with a jug for water to bathe old Joshua's eyes, or to give to the herb woman who came round each spring for a bottle of iron-water.

Susan and Becky could just see the yellow trough over the ridge and down the hill as they stood on the steps, a brightly coloured oasis in the green of the pasture, and the noise of the water came faintly across the field. A mare stood drinking, lifting her head and drinking again. Then she shook off the clinging drops, lifted her great hoofs out of the squelching mud, and walked towards them.

Becky took the key from her pocket and unlocked the door. She slipped a finger through the round hole in the upper half and lifted the latch. The chirps which they had heard all the time they gazed across the fields became frantic with excitement as they entered, but nothing could be seen at first.

Three large chambers, which spread over the cow-house, a barn, a cart-shed, and a store-room, lay before them. They were lighted at either end by windows, cobwebbed and dusty, it is true, but the cobwebs were delicate and grey and the dust was pearly. That to the south looked across a valley by the house and farm to the hills, and that to the north faced the groves of beech trees and the open calf-sheds, the far fields, and the hilly woods.

The chambers were separated by heavy stone archways and the curved roof with its oaken beams was like the roof of a Saxon church. Susan never got over the feeling of awe and mystery in the Three Chambers. The south window looked like the window over the altar in church and the sun streamed through, lighting up the fine particles of dust and white metal which for ever floated in the air, so that they were streams of gold.

There was a trap-door in the floor of one of the rooms which went into the barn below, through which the chop was poured. There was the wonderful chopping machine in the third chamber, with a belt through the floor and a horse walking round and round, like a circus pony, in the field below. She decorated him with blue streamers of vetch, and, with a wreath of daisies on her head, rode on his back, like the lady who jumped through the hoops.

There was the great empty space, the feeling of splendour up there, level with the tops of trees and haystacks. She skipped with a halter up and down without hindrance to show Becky what she could do. There was the smell of hay, and delicious oil-cake which was stored in long slabs in a corner.

There was danger here too, she was never allowed up alone, for two doors opened on to nothing whatever, and the trap-door in the floor had knives and a cutter underneath, whilst the chopping machine would cut her into little pieces if she went near.

But in the spring there was the added attraction of yellow downy chickens, which were kept here to be safe from hawks and rats for a few weeks. The hen-coops stood in the beams of the sun, and in front of each ran a score of chicks, chirping and chattering, unconscious of harm. Between the wooden bars peered anxious-eyed, stout, fluffy mothers, with warning, querulous voices full of cares. Becky fed them all and talked encouragingly to the hens, who refused to be pacified.

'There! There! Don't take on so! What ails you? I'm not going to eat your tiddly 'uns.'

'Hens are like women,' she said to Susan, 'too fussy over their little 'uns, never content, never settled. It's for all the world like a school treat with the mammies calling their childer, each one thinking her own's the best.'

Susan climbed down the stairs, with a hand on the wall to steady herself, and brought back a tin of water from the trough at the door of the cow-house, clean cool water for

ever trickling in the mossy trough at one corner and out at the other.

She could spend all day here, looking at the chicks, listening to the quietness of the Three Chambers, in which the chirps seemed like the voices of the choir-boys at church; but Becky had to go and Susan too had work to do. They closed and locked the door, leaving the glinting dust and the happy tiny creatures under the high arched roof.

As they walked through the stack-yards Becky stopped to hunt under the straddles. Sure enough there were some eggs, where a hen had strayed, the black slender hen, 'the Piece', who never did as she was bidden.

In the field where the cocks and hens wandered down to the little oak wood were some older chicks with their mothers. A brown hawk from the beech woods sailed overhead and hung motionless, a speck in the sky. But the hens saw her and screamed a warning to the mothers in the coops. The chickens ran with outstretched tiny wings, as the hawk swooped. Becky shouted, 'Shoo, shoo, shoo,' and clapped her hands, and Susan screamed. The hawk swerved away and soared up to the sky. Susan ran to tell her father.

He lifted his gun down, loaded it, and stood leaning over the wall like a grey shadow until the hawk returned.

A crack shivered the air and echoed against the buildings. The hawk fluttered and fell, turning over and over to the ground, for Tom never missed when he took up his gun.

He fetched a hammer and nail and hung it on a tree as a warning to other hawks who would see it and beware.

Afternoon came and milking-time. Dan and Becky flung open the gates of the farmyard and called the cattle. Tom wouldn't have them hurried and mithered with a sheep dog, who would chase round them and trouble their calm.

Young lambs played with each other, leaping in ecstasy, or buffeting with their knobby foreheads. The sheep lay under the velvet shadow of the black stone. Dan walked out into the field singing, 'Coo, coo, coo, coo-up, coo-up.' The cows in the distant field lifted their heads and listened, and then began to move slowly, eating as they came. 'Coo, coo, coo-up,' called Becky in her high voice. Susan ran down the fields, one, two, three fields away and opened all the gates.

Under the deep sunshine the cows walked in a procession across the fields, with great swinging udders full of milk, biting off clover and daisies as they passed through the wide-open gates, which Susan shut after them, up the hills, down the little valleys, now disappearing, now shining out with their satiny coats, across a stream, and under the trees to the farm.

Susan walked behind the last one, gently tickling her with a sycamore wand, which she peeled as she walked, to make a white stick. Suddenly the cow realized she was going to be the last. She started to run up the slope, and the others hurried too, hustling, pushing, like a lot of eager schoolgirls, each striving to be first at the gate.

Becky shut the gate after the first, in the faces of the others who looked at her with aggrieved gentle eyes.

'No, you don't, then. One at a time, my ladies,' she cried. She opened the gate so that two or three were admitted to the yard. They drank deep at the cow-trough, and then each returned to her own stall, where Joshua and Dan waited for them with the heavy chains which they hooked round their necks.

Joshua foddered them from the big barn into which their faces peeped through square openings in the walls. Susan ran along behind him, saying a word to each animal, patting its neck, rubbing its curly forehead, giving it an extra wisp of hay, and looking into its mournful eyes. She was sure they were talking to her, and she whispered back very low, so that no one could hear.

Tom Garland entered the yard with the heavy oaken yokes across his shoulders, walking with the swaying motion of those who have lived long days on the open hills. The shining empty pails, which Becky cleaned and rubbed each day, rattled together like bells, two on each side. He hung up his yoke on a nail outside, beside the men's yokes, and walked into the big cow-house.

'Come on, Susan,' he called. 'Where's the lass?'

'Here, Father, feeding the cows,' came Susan's voice from the barn.

'Come and make yourself useful. I want you to hold the cows' tails, flies are biting tonight.'

She obediently hurried into the cow-house, and stood on the raised path, facing the row of cows' tails, swishing backwards and forwards like pendulums. Tom Garland and Dan each sat on a four-legged oaken stool, milking, with their heads pressed against the cows' silky sides, and the can held between their knees. Joshua and Becky were in another cow-house, milking the meek-eyed Alderney and Jerseys.

Susan took a curly protesting tail-end in each hand and held on tightly. The cows stamped now and again and tried to swish their tails suddenly away, so she must never relax her grasp. Two swift streams of milk sang into each can, ding dong, ding dong, like little silver church bells. The white froth rose higher, and nobody spoke, for the cows liked peace and quietness when they were milked. They couldn't bear a loud noise, a sudden movement, or strange hands. Becky's voice could be heard singing, 'Shall we gather at the river'. Becky always sang, she said the cows gave more milk, and certainly they kept very still as if they were enjoying it as they yielded their milk to her hands with ease.

Tom sometimes whistled below his breath, a tiny sound, but soothing, and Dan chirruped and talked to the 'old girls'.

Susan gripped tightly till her fingers ached, as the cows twitched their tails. Flies settled on her face, and she could not drive them off; she was in the same fix as the cows, Tom said, when she complained, and must bear it.

Suddenly a tail slipped from her grasp and whacked Dan's face with a stinging lash.

'Here, come off there,' he cried angrily. 'What are you doing? Why don't you hold it tight?'

'I couldn't help it, Dan, it pulled away,' she answered, grabbing the tail again and standing well back, for one cow was a kicker and had sent the pail of milk on the floor more than once.

Then came the quiet stripping sound, tong, tong, tong. The bell had nearly ceased. The cans of frothing milk were hung up in a trough to cool before they went to the troughs by the house, and Susan stirred them round whilst the men got other cans for the next cows. She held more and more curly-ended tails, and her little legs were weary of standing so still, and her arms ached right up to the shoulders. She slipped away when her father entered the second cow-house, and went to watch Becky and Joshua.

Becky sang another hymn in time to the jets of milk which rang in her pail, and Joshua listened and thought of his young days when he sang like a lark, with carol-singers and chapel and at the Harvest Home, over sixty years ago. Now his voice was cracked, a tinkling pot.

Susan stopped a few moments, but any time she might

have more work to do, so she stepped out into the splendid sunshine, opened the gate softly, and ran down the fields.

In the hedges the chaffinches and tomtits sang their merry songs, shook their peals of bells, and tripped and fluttered their wings. She wished she had her triangle to add to the music, but it was in the house, hanging over the toasting-fork by the fire. She stood listening, trying to whistle in the same way. Then she stooped to the ground. Ferns with little folded hands waited to open. She uncurled one and tiny green fingers clasped hers, and dropped back again when she removed her hand. The knotted crab tree with its sloping, twisting trunk was full of pink bloom, and the hawthorn was out, long lines of May, like washing spread out on the hedge to dry.

She brought a branch down to her face and drank deep draughts of the almond smell, but she did not offer to pick any of the white speckled flowers. Instead she gathered the young bread-and-cheese, off the spiky twigs, and ate it with sour-dock and wood-sorrel from below the hedge. How delicious it was! She stayed her hunger with the sweet-sour tastes, and looked for birds' nests, just to peep and touch.

She remembered that when she was six she was just tall enough to reach the boughs of May. She had stood on tiptoe, in this very place, a little girl in a blue sun-bonnet, panting, excited to be so far from home alone, breaking off the sprays and tossing them on the ground.

'Won't Mother be pleased, all these pretty flowers. Won't Father be pleased! And Joshua. Everybody will be pleased with little Susan.'

She had gathered up the blossoms in her pinafore, scratching her arms with the thorns, but heedless as she thought of her mother's bright eyes. She ran home, with her short legs clambering up the steep hills, squeezing through the stiles, always holding her pinafore round her treasure. She crossed the meadow, out of breath, happy, intoxicated by the smell and her own cleverness. She peeped at the glory in her pinafore. It was all there, she hadn't lost one tiny bit of the creamy flowers starred with red.

She rushed hot and joyous to the south parlour where her mother sat sewing. She looked up surprised and smiling as Susan ran to her.

'Mother, Mother, Mother. Look what I've brought you. Pretty flowers.' Then a most bewildering thing happened which Susan could not even now explain. Her mother's smiles died away when she saw the flowers, and her face paled. Her eyes dilated in that special way, and Susan shrank back.

'Take them out this minute, this very second,' she cried, pushing Susan back through the hall and across the kitchen to the back door.

'Don't you know what they mean? Bad luck and worse. They mean death.'

Susan had stared, but the words remained.

'You must never, never, never bring those flowers in the house.' She threw them all away, over the wall, down the cliff, among the rabbit holes and clinging ivy.

Susan wept. It was worse than when she had picked all the geraniums from the garden that her father had just planted. Margaret nearly cried too, Joshua looked grave, and her father had said 'Dang' when he heard it.

They all knew people who had died within a year when May was brought into the house. So never again would Susan pick even one little flower, or she would be a murderer.

Instead she looked for lords and ladies. She opened their green hoods and peeped inside at the secret hidden ladies in their brown dresses. She always expected to find someone else there, the lord, perhaps, a face, a pair of brown eyes, a broad nose and a laughing mouth, but never had she found him. Every spring she hunted for that someone whom she could not discover, hiding in the strange mysterious green flowers.

CHAPTER 17

The Garden

SUSAN sat hiding on the damp moss-covered seat at the
end of the garden between the sage and the herb garden.
No one could see her there, for the bush of sage was like a
small tree, a sure sign that the farm was governed by petticoats, said Tom.

She had come to sit and think, about trees and God, and
hell, about animals talking and what was over the edge of
the world. She knew she should be in the house helping,
and she was deliberately sinning.

The kitchen-garden was a pleasant hiding-place, and one
in which she had never been found, for it was full of bushes
among which she could crouch unseen in her dark frock.
All round were fruit trees, black-currant bushes and red
currants alternately along the top border, for like everything else it was on a slope. There were large single roses,
bushes of fragrant cottage roses, behind them close to the
wall, and tall cherry and pear trees in between. Gooseberries grew along the other sides of the square, separated
from the thick hedge by flagged paths. There were little
hairy sweet gooseberries, great red globes which looked like
blood when they were held up to the light, smooth yellow
balloons filled with wine, such gooseberries as grew nowhere else, so old were the bushes, so gnarled and twisted.

Under a wall a bed of horse-radish spread its long leaves,
and under these grew white violets, dark velvety pansies,
and rich red polyanthus. 'Red cowslips' they called them,
for Tom said he grew them by planting roots of wild cowslips upside down.

Susan watched him do it once, and certainly the long-stalked lovely flowers which were in such request at school grew from that topsy-turvy root. Susan felt anything might happen in that garden, and she had planted pennies and date-stones, and upside down buttercups. Her mother ripened cream-cheese in the soil, buried deep in their little muslin cloths, the place marked with a stick. Often Susan had been sent to dig them up after the correct two or three days. Once the stick was lost and Dan spent half an hour digging for the missing cheese.

There were pink and red carnations, mignonette and musk, all growing among the fruit bushes. The rest of the flowers, the stocks and 'gillivers', the love-lies-bleeding and cock's comb, grannie's bonnets, and lark's spur, grew on the beds enclosed by the house-wall, round the monkey tree, among the box and 'rosy dandrums', under the windows of the parlours and stone room.

The garden itself was filled with rows of peas and beans, oblong beds of onion and carrot, lettuce and radish, celery and rhubarb. It was full to overflowing with fruit and vegetables, for however poor the fields might be, the garden was rich and prosperous.

Lilac hung over the gate, and nut trees swept the walls. There were scarecrows, traps, and nets, but the pheasants and rabbits came every day to take their toll.

Waves of wormwood, rue, and fennel spread round her, sharpening her senses, clearing her head with their bitter smells. Marjoram and sage were homely kitchen scents, but these others cast a chill over her as she looked at their dull leaves.

She thought of the trees she loved, the ancient yews, guarding the house, which she had never ventured to climb, for they were sacred and poison, and not to be trifled with. There were the ash trees, knee-deep in buttercups, delicate, unearthly, soft-moving, and the friendly beech trees with swings in their low boughs, and the hard-working apple trees in the orchard, which carried the clothes-lines full of fluttering white sheets, and held their blossom for the bees in spring, and were laden with green and yellow fruit in the autumn.

She thought of the fierce unfriendly trees in the wood, whispering and muttering. The ash trees there were cold and cruel, the elms were deformed, the oaks full of sinister things, secret, dark. Even the beeches concealed eyes and long-nailed fingers behind their trunks.

Then she wondered about animals talking. She could make everything understand, but not always could she get her answer. Animals' talk was silent, it came from their eyes, but the talk of things, of rooms and trees and fields came when she was very, very quiet and listened until they seemed to come alive. She was very happy to have all these friends.

Then she thought of enemies – the fox, one of the cows, an armchair, and Old Mother Besom, the witch.

'Susan! Susan! Susan!'

Margaret's voice thrilled all the garden and broke the silence into little pieces like splintering glass. Susan made an involuntary movement of obedience and repressed it.

'Susan! Susan! Come and peel the potatoes.'

Steps were approaching across the grass, the garden gate banged and Mrs Garland hurried down the path. She stooped to pick some thyme and a bunch of parsley bordering the stones. Then she sighed deeply and went out again.

Susan sat very still. She looked up at the sky. The morning air was sweet with the smell of the great woods which were only a few yards away, over the wall and across a dell. Little clouds looked like the petals of one of the roses on the house.

And did God live up there? But He was here too, in the garden, and she was sinning. God had seen her, His eye saw everything. Then He would know she didn't want to peel the potatoes, not today. She would go to hell if she died now, but if she lived till she had said her prayers to-night she would be safe once more. Suppose God struck her dead for her sin, and she dropped down among the rue and fennel. She looked down at her buttoned boots and wondered if she would have time to tuck them under her. Boots didn't look nice, sticking out like the cow's legs. But no one would ever find her here, no one came to the end of the garden unless they were having roast pork. It would be a long time to wait, she had better say a prayer now.

She closed her eyes, put her hands together, and sat with the sun beating in hot waves on her eyelids.

One year, when Mr and Mrs Garland had gone for their seaside holiday they asked a dour good woman named Deborah to take charge of the house and look after Susan. Debby had been converted and she spent the evenings trying to turn Dan and Becky in the right way. Becky was quickly persuaded, but Dan was more obstinate and curious.

Susan sat in the kitchen one night, playing with her doll, drawing crooked houses and long horses on backs of envelopes, and cutting out the fashions in a journal. Becky was out and Debby took the chance to describe hell and all its torments to Dan, who sat open-mouthed with his arms on the table.

'Gypsy Bill says the world will come to an end before another year's out,' she continued. 'Old Moore prophesies the same, it's in his almanack.' She went to the dresser drawer and took out Old Moore to find the very passage. Susan gave all her attention to the conversation; books were true, Old Moore was Bible truth.

'They say Queen Victoria believes the end is near, too. There are all the signs – drinking, evil living, war – and there's been a bright star seen, what they call a comet. It will strike the earth and burn it up. Then the dead will rise, and the good will go up to Life Everlasting, but the wicked will go down to Everlasting Fire.'

'Is there a trough in hell?' asked Susan.

Deborah started. 'You go off to bed. I didn't notice you were sitting up so late,' she said sternly, and reaching a candlestick she lighted it and hurried Susan through the door and upstairs to her crib. But as she shut the door she said, 'Little girls had better prepare their souls', and Susan had never spoken of her fears. She had lain awake – she was only six – afraid for hours, expecting the bedroom floor to collapse and the house to fall like the walls of Jericho.

Susan had never forgotten that night, nor the following days when she waited for the end of the world, and listened for the great trump sounding through the woods, across the fields, frightening the cattle who would fall into pits in the earth. The soft grass, the flowers, the trees, covered a frightful hell, all raging and burning in the ground, half-way to Australia.

When the New Year had passed and the world was still alive she found that Deborah and Queen Victoria had made a mistake in the date. But any time it might come, and she was still expecting it.

'Wherever have you been, Susan?' exclaimed her mother when she entered the house. 'Come and peel the potatoes at once. I called you long ago. It's very wrong and wicked to be disobedient.'

So the potatoes were still waiting. She fetched clean water from the trough and stood over the slop-stone. Potato peeling was no fun when people were near, but when she was alone she talked to each one. She heard the little potato voices calling, 'Me next, me next,' as they pushed to get into her hands, to have their brown coats removed. Today neither she nor the potatoes spoke, but she gave them a nod of recognition so that they would know who peeled them.

There was an uncomfortable feeling in the house, nobody spoke, and disasters and sorrows hung in the air. Susan felt it was her naughtiness, and prepared for a punishment.

Tom came downstairs in his best clothes, and Margaret brushed his large square hat. Dan came in to say the trap was ready, and Becky got the whip.

'Where is Father going?' asked Susan.

'To the milkman,' answered Margaret, with a sigh. 'He hasn't paid for months, and we heard this morning he's gone bankrupt.'

Bankruptcy! The same thing had happened before. Susan didn't know what it meant, except that it took the sweetness from her mother's life.

It was a quiet unhappy day. Susan went off, stone-picking with Joshua all the afternoon. They roamed the fields, up and down, with baskets on their arms, weaving patterns as they picked up stones which might injure the scythes when the grass was cut.

Where they all came from no one knew. Joshua said they grew, for he had cleared grass year after year for nigh on sixty years, and still there were stones. Perhaps they were the spawn of the black stone, the strange menhir by the house, he wouldn't be surprised.

They poured them in heaps, and Joshua gathered all together and carried them away to fill up the holes in the cart roads. It would take days to clear all the fields, but Dan and Becky would help.

The fields looked cold and grey. Sadness like a dove brooded over them. The sun went down and a chill wind came from behind the northern hills, sweeping the trees aside, making white tracks on the grass as it blew past the farm to the valley.

Dan and Joshua went milking, and Susan collected the eggs, and counted them into the great brown market baskets ready for the next day. Becky scalded the wooden churn ready for butter-making if the rumour were true, and the milk had to be kept at home. Margaret sat sewing, turning and mending, with deep sighs and troubled glances at the clock.

At night they sat by the fire, Joshua and Dan cutting spelds, Becky making door-mats from pieces of heavy cloth, Margaret finishing a patchwork quilt for Joshua's bed, a pattern of prints, lavenders, and pinks, cut into little squares and joined together. Eight o'clock struck, Dan harnessed the pony and went down to the station. Susan wanted to sit up to hear what had happened, but she was sent quickly to bed.

The dog barked, the gate banged with a loud clamour, and the pony and the trap drove up to the house.

Margaret ran out.

'What news, Tom? What does he say?'

'Nothing. It's domino,' replied Tom heavily, as he climbed down and walked into the house with rug and whip. 'We must find a new milkman and begin again, but honest ones are as hard to find as roses in winter.'

The noise and din of the town still ringing in his ears, the laughter and bitter words, died away in the night, the peace of the hills and open fields soothed and quietened him as he lay awake in the oak chamber.

No churns rattled along the paved paths the next day, nor for a few weeks, and the milk train left without its load from Windystone Hall. But Windystone was not the only farm caught in the bankruptcy. Snow of Bluebell End Farm and Jonathan Wild of Inglenook lost their money too. Jonathan was already in deep water, and he sold up and went to America, but Snow, like Tom Garland, sold some cattle to keep going, and made butter till he found a new dealer.

CHAPTER 18

The Oatcake Man

BECKY was a good hand at butter-making. She turned the handle of the churn, and coaxed the fine yellow grains together to make the solid lump, with a murmur of magic words. Susan hovered near, but she was not allowed to touch, for sometimes an elfish spirit gets in the churn and only those with the charm can get the butter to come. So she muttered and mumbled alone, and sure enough the sound of the swish, swish, altered, little animal thuds were heard, and the miracle happened.

Then came the patting and moulding, the squeezing and pressing, and the cool clean smell, as Margaret deftly shaped the butter with the wooden prints which had floated in the trough all day. The squares and rounds with bold solid English designs were packed in green leaves and sent to the shops, and Becky began the next batch.

She was a hardy, weather-beaten, good-tempered girl, with cheeks as firm and red as apples, and eyes brown as ripe hazel nuts. She was as strong as a man, and could carry a young calf in her arms, or two brimming cans of milk with anybody. She could wash, bake, brew herb beer, harness the horses, milk the cows, and take a turn in the fields.

Dan was for ever teasing her, but she bore it all with cheerful grins. He told her that the farm lads were in love with her, that the barber had asked for a lock of her hair, and that the road-mender was waiting down on the road, sitting on a heap of stones for a glimpse of her.

She shook her head and repeated:

'Nobody doesna want me, I reckon, but Mr Right will come some day,' and she washed up the milk-cans and scalded the churns, and polished the little brass labels, planning in the meantime a new ribbon for her neck to wear the next time she went out.

She rubbed the great copper pan, filled it with clean water and set it on the stove. She gave the dog his breakfast and patted him as he fed from the bowl. She dipped into the deep painted bin for 'Indy corn' and threw the grain to the flock of hens and cocks, clustering in reds and browns and gold on the cobbled stones before the barn door. Always she kept an eye open for the hen with a drooping wing, the sad-eyed white hen which always fed alone, and the speckled hen which limped, the strays and outcasts of the poultry-yard.

She treated the cows as friendly human beings, slapping them on the back, joking with them, singing to them, scolding them if they were rough or unmannerly, full of praise when they were in a good humour. Only the bull she avoided, since she had been chased through the cattle-yard. His smouldering red eyes and deep breathing remained in her memory.

She suckled the young calves, the jostling crowd of big-eyed youngsters. There was a new cow-calf, a little red beauty, a daughter of the pedigree Maiden of Minn. All night Susan had heard the dull moaning and lowing of a cow in pain. It disturbed her sleep, and her mother came up to her.

'It's the red cow calving, it's Maiden. She's very poorly, and Father and Joshua are sitting up all night with her. Now go to sleep. There'll be a Suckey Mull in the morning, please God.'

She hurried downstairs to make up a bed for one of the men on the settle, and Becky made gruel for the cow, and got the drinking-horn from the stone chamber, and the medicines. She put the teapot on the hob and left a big fire ready for the night's vigil.

In the morning Susan awoke to see cloud shadows chasing across the fields. She tried to remember what the exciting thing was. She dressed hastily and jumped downstairs two at a time in a new way she had discovered.

'Is there a Suckey Mull?' she asked as she ran to her mother.

'Yes, a cow-calf, thank God, a good one, strong and big,' replied Margaret, kissing her. Tom Garland came in to make a red drink for Maiden whose life had hung in the balance.

When Susan went to the calf place, there in a nest of hay in the stall lay a small, damp, red, curly-haired little calf, with shapely head and white face and body like a fawn's.

Susan climbed up the door and leaned over to look at the sweet-smelling, slobbering, astonished creature. She held out her fingers and the calf struggled to its feet, bumping its head against the wooden walls of the stall.

'Coom up, coom up, Suckey Mull,' crooned the child, as she slipped her fingers into its warm mouth. As it sucked she scratched its knobby head with the little horns hidden under the curls, and talked to the unsteady animal.

Becky would teach it to drink from the can the rich milk of its mother. She had a way with animals and they trusted her completely. She mothered the cade lamb which was left an orphan at birth in the early spring. She carried it to the kitchen, with endearing talk, and gave it warm milk from the suckling-can as it lay a helpless curly-haired baby, with black knobbly legs and soft mouth. It nuzzled up to her and baaed piteously when she put it out in the barn. For weeks it stayed a Peter Pan lamb, and Susan spent many hours feeding the little one in the orchard, racing with it, butting it. Its tail wagged like a crazy pendulum as it drained the can, pushing Susan against the apple trees as it endeavoured to get more than the last drop.

Little pigs, the Anthonys, left out in the cold by a callous mother, chickens which had been trodden on by a careless hen, ducklings and young turkeys, all came to the kitchen and lay on the rug in front of the fire, or in flannel-lined baskets, as they struggled to get a hold on life. Becky coaxed life back into them, holding them in her warm hand, when they lay with eyes closed, twitching feet, and tiny hearts scarcely beating.

'Little tiddly things,' she said. 'I feel that sorry for them. Their mothers are like a woman I once knowed, thinking of nothing but pleasuring herself, and leaving her childer to get on as best they could.'

She wiped her hands on her apron and looked down on

the yellow balls straddling unsteadily in the basket. She clattered down the wet paths with her iron pattens over her shoes, among rose trees and ferns which drenched her with raindrops, carrying pails of swill and hot meal for the sows and their litters, through the yellow gate and into the thicket of purpling lilac and white-flowered elderberry. As soon as they heard her step the pigs started to squeal with greediness and excitement. She poured the food through the openings in the wall with its roof of stone-crop and house-leek, down into the ancient troughs.

'You're a bad thing,' she scolded the sow, 'to leave your Anthony out in the cold. Just take care of him now he's well again.'

One day Becky was alone in the house, busy with a dozen

things at once. A couple of chicks chirped in the basket on the hearth, and a blackbird with a broken wing set with a little splint pecked from a saucer of sop. The smell of baking came in waves from the oven where Becky crouched, with her oven cloth, putting in a fresh batch. She took out the brown loaves and turned them upside down out of their tins. She tapped on the bottoms listening with her head on one side, as if she expected a little bread man to open the door of the loaf and walk out to her.

'I wish Mr Right would come along quick,' she thought as she placed the loaves in a row, and cut fresh lumps from the remaining dough to 'prove' on the rack over the oven.

A knife fell on the floor, and she picked it up. That was a sign a man was coming. If it had been a fork, a woman would be expected. A black soot had waved on the bar all the afternoon, a stranger was on the way. She took off her floury apron and put on a clean one. She straightened up the kitchen and tidied her hair. Then she went to the little looking-glass which hung on the wall, and gazed intently at herself. Rosy cheeks, brown eyes, thick brown hair, a large mouth. She sighed, 'I wish I wasn't so red, red hands and cheeks. Vinegar makes a body pale, but I can't abide the stuff.' She sighed and absent-mindedly broke off a piece of kissing crust which she laid aside for Susan, when she returned from school.

Roger barked and tugged at his chain, and she heard steps coming to the side door. It was the oatcake man; she was glad she had heeded the signs and redded up.

'Come in, Mister,' she cried when she saw him, and he entered the low door and took off his cap. He put his large basket, with its neat piles of brown oatcakes and cream honeycombed pikelets all covered with a white cloth, on the dresser end, and stood shyly by the door.

'You've got quite a family, Miss,' said he. Bright blushes flooded Becky's neck and mounted to her forehead. She felt cross with herself for reddening; she and Susan were cautions for blushing at nothing.

'Them's been badly,' she explained, 'and I'm taking care of them. Missus and master are out driving, and the little girl is at school. Will you have a cup of tea? You've walked a fair way.'

'Thank you kindly, I will,' said the young man. 'My basket's a tidy weight, and it's a good pull up this hill.'

Becky pulled out a chair for him and left him by the fire, whilst she went to the cupboard for cups and saucers and the tea. She gave the big copper kettle a shake as it sat on the fire, which seemed to wake it from a sleep, for it immediately began to sing. Then she went to the dairy for milk. She came back with a little jug perched like a bird on one crooked finger.

'A drop of cream, Mister? It wouldn't be amiss, would it?'

'I don't mind a speck, I never say nay to a good thing, and not much cream comes my way,' answered the oatcake man, as he stooped over the chicks.

Becky set the table and made the tea, keeping a wary eye on the man whom she had never seen without a hat. He was long-legged, tall and straight, curly-haired like the lambs, with a fresh open face and blue eyes. He had only one arm and his empty sleeve was pinned with a large safety-pin to his coat.

'Draw up to the table, Mister,' said Becky. So he drew up his chair with a squeak over the floor and sat down opposite Becky, who felt abashed and proud of her boldness. Here she was sitting in the missus's place, and he was in the master's. What had come over her?

'A drop of tea is very welcome,' he said, as he drained the cup at a draught and passed it back to Becky. She blushed and refilled it, with a good supply of thick cream, and plenty of brown sugar.

'Was it sweet enough, Mister?' she asked demurely.

'Aye, I've got a sweet tooth, but it was grand.'

'We're all fond of plenty of sugar,' said Becky, and she waited a second to see if he would return the obvious compliment which everyone gave, 'You don't need sugar, you are sweet enough without,' but the oatcake man did not reply.

He was framing his next remark.

'What do they call you, Miss?'

'Becky,' she said, 'Becky Moss. I'm an orphan, and I've lived here three year come Michaelmas. It's a good place, but hard.'

'It's a nice name, Becky,' he said, as he ate hungrily at the crusty new bread and butter. 'Becky short for Rebecca I suppose.' Becky noticed that his cheeks were thin and he ate as if he had had little to eat that day.

'What's *your* name, Mister?' she ventured.

'Gabriel Thorn,' he answered. 'I live at Downton, along with my mother. She's a widow-woman. My father was killed at the quarry. He was a quarryman at Great Hop Quarry; a stone fell on him and crushed him dead. That was a bad business.'

'It was, I am sorry,' replied Becky sympathetically. 'And how did you lose your arm,' she continued, filling his cup again. 'Did you work in the quarry too?'

'No, I've been a sailor, but I had this accident, so I had to give up and come home. Now I sell the oatcakes and my mother makes them.'

'That reminds me, I'll buy tuthree. Give me a dozen of both, Mister Thorn,' she smiled.

'Nay, call me Gabriel, everyone does,' said the young man politely, as he rose and wiped his mouth. 'Thank you very kindly for the tea,' he said, and Becky sedately answered:

'You're very welcome.'

He put out the batches of the thin cakes, and, readjusting the clean cloth (which Becky could see his old mother washing and hanging on the garden hedge and ironing), he hitched the basket with its broad leather strap on to his shoulder, and went off.

Becky walked down the little lavender path to the small

gate with him and stepped across the cobbles in the yard
towards the big gate in the drive, pretending to be looking
for the trap.

She waved when he turned his head as he disappeared
round the corner among the crimsoning mallows, and he
nodded back.

She returned excited and laughing to the kitchen. She had
known she would have a sweetheart because the thorny
briars had clung to her skirts down the lane.

'What a nice young man. And so polite. Took his cap off
when he came in, and him with only one arm, and called
me Miss, and didn't sit down till he was asked, and didn't
drink out of his saucer. Quite the gentleman! What a good
thing I noticed the stranger on the bar and changed myself.'

She sang as she washed up. 'Above the bright blue sky',
and 'A fair country maid'. She had just gone into 'There is
a happy land', when Roger barked again, and the blackbird piped, and the chickens chirped, and the door flew open
to admit Mrs Garland laden with string bags and parcels
and the weekly paper.

'Take that blackbird away before it gets trodden on,
Becky,' she cried, 'and move the chicks, and make the tea;
your master's here. There's a piece of steak to cook, and a
tea-cake to toast.'

Becky ran out for the rugs and whip, and raced into
pantry and larder for food and dishes.

A quarter of an hour later the kitchen was full of noise
and chatter, of good savoury smells, of tea and meat, of
toast and cake, of sizzling and bubbling, of tramping feet
and loud-breathing men. Joshua came in from putting the
horse in the stable, Dan came through to see the time, on
his way to the milking. Mrs Garland opened her parcels,
put away the groceries, counted the butter and egg money,
and sat down to tea.

Then Susan came in, flushed and early – they had come
out half an hour earlier as the school was wanted for a

lecture, and the children had scampered home to surprise their parents.

'The oatcake man's been this afternoon, and I bought two batches,' said Becky, flushing, 'and he will wait for the money till he calls next time. I gave him a cup of tea, he looked that tired. His name's Gabriel, he told me, Gabriel Thorn, and he's been a sailor, and he has only one arm.'

'You've been busy while we've been away,' commented the farmer drily.

'You shouldn't ask anyone in when we are out, Becky, it isn't proper. Don't do it again. I don't mind a meal at the door, but not inside when we are away,' and Margaret pursed her lips and shook her head.

Susan looked from one to the other, and then stared at Becky's blushing face. She made up her mind to look at this Gabriel who had been a sailor.

Tea continued in silence, for however much noise and clatter went in the preparation, Tom liked quiet whilst he fed. Margaret sat wrapped in her thoughts, Becky dreamed as she got ready the men's tea, but Susan looked at the clock and nodded to the dresser, and talked her silent talk as she ate her bread soaked in gravy, and her 'Matrimony and Sorrow begins'.

When she and Becky were alone she got the whole story out of her.

'If you marry him, Becky, I shall come and see you, and nurse your babies. We will buy lots of oatcakes and pikelets, and you will have to make them as well as his mother. Perhaps he could live here and be a cowman.'

'He won't have me, Susan, I'm not clever enough for him, I've had no schooling. I was thinking about it when you had tea. I went to work when I was ten, for I couldn't understand school ways and my mother was always ailing,' said Becky despondently.

'I'll teach you at nights, Becky. You could learn to read and spell and write.' Susan's eyes shone and she clasped and unclasped her fingers.

Every night when the milking was finished, and the tea things were cleared away, Becky got out her copy-book. With infinite pains and long deep sighs, her shining head of glossy hair nearly touching the table, and her tongue poking out first at one corner and then at the other corner of her mouth, she copied 'Adversity, Avarice, Amity'. Susan hung over her, encouraging, praising, and dotting her i's. Joshua was pleased at her efforts, but Dan laughed and tried to guess the reason. She carried a blue-backed spelling book in her pocket and spent odd minutes learning the list of words as she washed up and made the beds.

Susan felt that she too must add to her learning to keep her superior position. On the bookcase in the south parlour, wedged between *Plate-swimming*, *The Ladder to Learning*, and *Clarke's Wonders* was an old leather-bound Latin Grammar, which had belonged to some ancestor with a leaning towards knowledge.

She had heard at school that Latin was the universal language, and she wondered if she could converse more easily with the moon, or the furniture. Especially when she saw a whole page about a table, she determined to learn all about it, so she struggled with Mensa, with the book propped against a flower-pot on the window-sill as she peeled the potatoes. Everything would understand quite easily if she knew Latin.

So the revival of learning began, on the high slopes under the beech woods, in the fields, in barns and cow-sheds, in attic and kitchen. Susan addressed the rooms and trees with some words in their own tongue, and Becky's large round handwriting lay about on scraps of envelopes, with the O's carefully closed with little latches, and the T's bolted and barred.

The oatcake man came again, quite unconscious of the upheaval he had occasioned in the farm. He leaned against the doorpost and uncovered the basket of curling oatcakes and pale gold pikelets.

'Here's the oatcake man, Missus,' cried Becky, running in

from the garden with a handful of parsley and a bunch of rhubarb in her arms. She turned shyly to the man with flaming cheeks.

'Good morning, Mr Thorn, it's a grand day, isn't it?'

''Tis indeed,' agreed Gabriel, and he looked up at the great white cauliflower clouds which climbed from the hills to the top of the elm tree, clouds which might drench him before he got home, which might send shafts of lightning when he was over the ridge, but which were his companions on his long round between hamlet, farm, and distant village.

'How's the master, Mam?' he asked politely, as Margaret turned over his pikelets and handed out a bundle to Becky.

'Pretty middling, he has a touch of sciatica,' replied Margaret, feeling in her full gathered skirts for her purse.

'Ah,' replied Gabriel, 'I know a cure for that. Tell him to carry a little bottle of quicksilver in his hip pocket, Mam, and he'll be cured in a week.'

Margaret thanked him, she had heard of the remedy and would try it. But Becky's mind was revolving as fast as it was capable in an effort to find something to say now the man was before her. She was tongue-tied, and it looked as if he would go without a word if she wasn't quick.

'I've been writing a bit to fill in my time,' she said. ('God forgive me for the lie,' she whispered to herself.) 'Would you like to see?' and before he could answer she took her copybook from the drawer in the table and handed it to him.

'Love, loneliness, laughter,' he read.

'That's fine,' he exclaimed as he held it out and examined the letters. He looked at Becky. It was the first time he had seen her closely, for in the kitchen the light was always dim. He saw the tiny gold hairs shining on her strong arms, the soft bloom of her cheeks, her bright eyes, and her unwrinkled brown skin, smooth as a Dorking's egg.

He handed the book back to her, and took the money from Mrs Garland.

He said 'Good day', and walked down the path, through

the wicket gate and across the cobbled courtyard to the big gate. He went slowly down by the orchard, whistling softly, staring at the great rooted ivy which climbed along the old wall, a regular tree with boughs and branches.

'Mister Thorn,' cried a voice, 'Gabriel!' He turned sharply and Becky was leaning over the wall, looking down at him and waving to him to stop.

She ran through the gate and down the hill with something behind her back.

'I thought, leastways Missus thought, you might like a flower or two for your mother, seeing as how we have so many,' and she thrust into his basket three red roses which she had hastily plucked from the tree on the stable wall, and a spray of lad's love.

He smiled a rare smile and she ran back, not waiting to hear what he said.

The courting had begun, slow love-making, inarticulate with gifts of flowers and peppermints. They met sometimes in the leafy lanes, and wandered up the fields on Sunday nights, and spoke a few words at the door. Becky had done her share, and it was for him to be the pursuer, her boldness left her now she had found her man.

CHAPTER 19

Mowing-Time

SUMMER was coming, for long ago the first cuckoo had called in the ash tree, and Becky and Margaret had turned their money and wished. The cottage gardens were full of flowers, blue and purple grannie's bonnets, blue-eyed beauties, cabbage roses, and bachelor's buttons. The children took posies to school, lad's love and dark pansies squeezed tightly in their little hot hands. Susan gathered the cream-hearted tea roses heavy with scent which covered the gable of the house and spread under many windows. She exchanged them with the little girls, a rose for three pansies, a golden ball and a bleeding heart, or she left the little bunch on the teacher's desk, as a peace-offering.

It was the time for peep-shows, 'A pin to see a peep-show'. The children cut open a door from an envelope, and hid behind a piece of glass a few flower-petals arranged in a design, a group of slender leaves of lad's love, with a circle of larkspur petals. The payment to see the wonder, to lift the paper curtain and peep, was a pin. Susan carried a little round pincushion of money, and held in her hand a show of treasures from the pastures, the tiniest of daisies, with honey spots, tormentil, and wild pansies, tied with a grass.

The turnpike was thick with soft satiny dust, through which the children dragged their happy little boots, kicking up the powder to their noses. But their mothers, returning to their homes with heavy baskets of groceries, had creamy hems on their black skirts as if they had trailed them through milk. Millions of bluebells pushed their little white heads through the green rosettes in the Dark Wood, and rose on pale stems which deepened in a day, the lovely bells

drooped their heads and the bluebells were out, a sea beating against the trees, sweeping under the walls into the
fields far away. Taller and taller they grew, and their thick
stems curved like a sickle with the weight of the flowers.
A heavy scent filled the air, and bees awakened the silence
of the wood with a continuous hum.

Susan gathered armfuls of flowers in the fields near the
Dark Wood, and carried them a-tiptoe along the stony
path, never stopping to pick even the most splendid long-
stalked truss of flowers, the kings and queens, for in spring
the trees were wide awake and danger lurked again after
the winter rest. The woods which had been white with
snow were now blue with bluebells, the only flowers that
grew there, save filmy fumitory and the field of ragwort.

But in the friendly woods round Windystone Hall the
bluebells flourished and spilled over the edges, drifting
down the fields even to the gates of the house, lakes of blue,
mists in the deep green.

Swallows and swifts returned
to the farm, and the old nests
in the rafters of the cart places
and open sheds, and under the
eaves of the barn, were inhabited again. They brought good
luck and their clayey nests were
left undisturbed year after year.

But the colour of the bluebells deepened, the scent became
unbearably rich, the flowers bowed and swayed like swing-
boats at a fair as the bees plundered them. They faded,
green seeds peeped through the curled-back petals, and an
army of green soldiers laden with pointed knapsacks filled
the woods.

The grass became mowing-grass, not to be entered, however bright the flower or brilliant the butterfly. The fields
were red with ripening sorrel which spread above the grass
like a crimson net. The meadows were painted with rich
flowers, big white dog-daisies raising their wide-awake

faces to the sky, bright enamelled buttercups, clumps of blue and purple wild geranium, gold hawkweed on stilts peeping above the tall grass, lavender scabious, and elusive ragged robin.

Above the flowers flitted butterflies, and honey bees, clumsy bumble bees, and shining hoverflies. Deep down in the grass was another world, a dwarf world, a forest of small daisies and clover and tormentil with their attendant beasts, field mice, ants, green beetles, and wandering hedgehogs.

But on the hilltops where the grass was always thin, where no springs watered the soil, and the sun beat down on the rocks and boulders, the flowers were different. Here were little blue scabious, and bird's foot, poor man's weather glass, and yellow rattle.

The long slender grasses were full of games for children, the country child's toy shop, with millions of puzzle boxes waiting for little hands to play with them.

There were tinker tailor grasses, with their little green ears which told her fortune, tinker, tailor, soldier, sailor, or this year, next year, sometime, never, or silk, satin, muslin, rags.

There were pussy grasses whose green fur stripped off between her fingers and thumb, until a curly rib remained, which she twisted in Becky's hair, pulling until Becky called out, 'You're lugging me, Susan,' for, like an unmanageable curling pin, it wouldn't come out.

There were quaking grasses which nodded their little green and brown heads if she whispered near them, and rattled their heads in a box when the wind passed over.

There were delicate brown grasses which grew in hot woods among bilberry bushes, and carried strings of blue berries for her when she had no basket, and cock's foot, feathery and plumy, whose blades made mouth-organs and squeakers, and timothy grass which made a cudgel.

There was golden grass which lasted till Christmas in the Staffordshire jug in the parlour, and black-headed plantains which called out for a game of soldiers.

There were seed-boxes to be popped, and pods to be rifled, dandelion clocks to tell the time, and green rushes to be plaited into whips, or to be peeled for making ivory baskets and white roses.

Susan wandered up and down the field paths, playing with the field toys, and hunting for the giant kex which Dan would cut to make a whistle or a musical pipe. Every day was full of happiness and every night brimmed with beauty, but the farm waited, waited, growing ripe for the harvest.

One morning the post-boy brought a dirty letter with the postmark of a far-away village in County Galway. He carried it through the wood at seven o'clock in the morning and sat on a chair by the fire whilst Tom Garland slowly turned it over and then slowly opened it.

HONOURED SIR (it began),
    Will you kindly lend me the loan of a sovereign so as I can come to England for the harvesting.
    With best respects to the mistress,
Your humble servant
MICHAEL SULLIVAN

It was the usual request from Old Mike for his passage money from Ireland.

'Hurrah, hurrah, the Irishmen are coming,' shouted Susan, dancing excitedly round the table.

'Hold your whist,' cried Tom, 'I can't hear myself think.' He drew his leather bag from out of his deep trouser pocket, untied the string, and laboriously took out a sovereign. Margaret wrote a note to the post office and one to the Irishman. Then she wrapped up the sovereign in tissue paper and sealed it in an envelope, for the boy to take back with him.

'And mind you don't lose it,' she warned, as she gave him an apple for his trouble.

'They're rum folk, the Irish,' said Tom to Joshua, as they

sat over breakfast when the milk had gone and the house was peaceful again. There was, however, a wave of excitement in the room, a thrill, as if even the chairs rejoiced the Irishmen were coming, and the harvest, the culmination of the year's preparation, was approaching.

'They're rum folk. They say things back'ards road in their country. Why, once Mike was going to send a sovereign home to his wife in Ireland, and what do you think he wrote? He said, "Dear Wife, I'm going to send you a sovereign. Have you got it yet?" As if she could get it before he'd sent it! They go to church on Sunday mornings, they call it Mass, and then they've finished with religion for the day. They dance and sing at night, only up to twelve of the clock do they keep Sunday. It's heathen, that is. Dancing and singing on Sunday. But you know they worship idols in their religion, the Roman religion.'

Susan sat with open eyes and ears, listening, astonished. Whatever they did, everybody loved them, they knew no better.

'They don't talk the same as us,' Tom continued, 'and they're very touchy. You have to be main and careful how you deal with them. But they are good workers, I'd never have an English haymaker when I could get an Irishman.

'I remember once a swarm of bees went up to yon sycamore tree, the one by the garden wall, and one of the Irish, Dominick's father it was, he's been dead many a year, for I was only a little one same as Susan, he said he would get it for us. So up he goes and climbs along the bough to the swarm that hung there like a great pudding. We all stood watching him down below on the lawn there. He got the skep under them, but the bees swarmed all over him. They fair covered him in a black dust as it might be.

'Didn't he shout! He said "Bring the gun and shoot them. They'll pick me two eyes out, master."

'Well, the rest of the Irish, they laughed till their sides split, and we laughed too, I can tell you, but 'twas no laughing matter, for he was that swollen when he came down he couldn't do any work. We had to blue-bag him from head to foot.

'Mr Gladstone wants to give them Home Rule, but what would they do? They'd bring the Pope here in no time!'

Susan imagined a tall man, as tall as the beech trees, stalking in.

Everybody turned out to get the Irishmen's Place ready. It was a cow-house in the old buildings, near the stable, in the wing that overlooked the courtyard, a place kept for sick cows, and for cows in calf. When Tom bought a heifer he put her there to get used to things, to settle down before she joined the cows in a big cow-house, where she would be as nervous as a new child at school, he said.

The walls were a yard thick, and a cobbled path came up to the door, but bright grass stretched away along its outer walls, leading to rose trees and little bushes on which the Irish could dry their clothes.

Next to it was the cart-shed with great double doors and cupboards in the thickness of the walls. Near by was a mounting-block and a grassy bank with a lichened wall from which white rock fell in a sheet of blossom so that there was a continuous murmur of bees.

There were stalls for two cows, and an open space beyond, partitioned off by an oak screen, where some potatoes were stored for the winter. These were now removed and the place swilled. The wooden wall between the two stalls was rubbed smooth and polished like a mirror by cows rubbing their necks up and down through the long weary nights of pain. The window was a narrow slit in the thick wall, like the loop-holes in old castles, through which a shaft might be winged down the valley at a marauding foe, but now it was stuffed with a bag, for enough light and air came from the door which stood with its top-half open all day long.

The building was swept clean with besoms by Dan and Joshua, and then they lime-washed the walls. Five or six bags of fresh straw were laid on the floor at the back behind the partition. These were the beds in the Irishmen's bedroom, ready for the hot sweating men to fling themselves down, half undressed, and sleep the heavy drugged sleep of the field worker, the heavy dreamless sleep of bees in a hive.

It was gloomy behind there, and the rats scuffled away when footsteps approached. If the rat-catcher could come along before the Irish, so much the better, but Tom fastened the little hole through which they entered and kept them out.

The cow-stalls formed the living-room, the light half-room into which the sun shone all day. Here Dan and Joshua brought two long wooden forms and a round oaken table, marked by innumerable mugs, for it had been the Irishmen's table for generations. Several milking-stools, an iron cooking-pot, a pile of old willow-pattern plates and dishes, a pewter salt and pepper pot, some mugs and iron spoons completed the furniture of the Irishmen's Place.

Tom Garland carefully hung their picture, an oblong wooden tablet with 'NO SMOKEING ALOWED' painted on it in rough characters of a hundred years before. Fire was the dread of every farmer, for the water supply was scanty, although the streams were so many, and no fire-engine could get up those hills. A fire would mean absolute ruin, and Tom took every precaution against it. His own men never smoked, candlesticks had their extinguishers, and all lamps and lanterns were carefully guarded.

The Irishmen had one candle which was stuck on the spike in a tall iron candlestick, and fastened to the wall, but usually they sat outside in the starlight till they tumbled into bed.

Tom and Dan fetched all the rakes and two-pronged forks from the corner where they had been stacked for the winter, and laid them out on the Daisy Bank. The long scythes were lifted down from the barn walls, and honed until they gleamed in the playing sunlight which filtered through the overhanging elms. New teeth were made and fitted in the wooden rakes.

'Come along to the dentist,' called Tom, who loved his yearly joke. 'Come along and have some new teeth,' and Joshua laughed and pointed to his own toothless mouth.

Forks had new 'stails' made for them, and everything was overhauled and strengthened.

They were taken back to the barn and ranged in a row, with the scythes hung again on the wooden pins projecting from the high walls, over the enormous corn-bins, deep in the shadows.

In another barn a barrel of beer stood waiting, softly dripping into a brown jug, the only sound except the patter of rats and mice, unsettled by the upheaval in the Irishmen's Place. It stood on a pile of big stones, leaning against the whitewashed wall, with golden straw littered across the floor, all browns and creams, in the streaks of light which peeped in through the round thumb-hole in the door. Susan loved the smells in this barn, and the sound of the dripping beer, but more than all she liked the clear note of the brown stream when Becky filled a jug for the Irishmen. It was music like the tinkle of the triangle, and the song of the linnets in the orchard, and the chaffinch in the plum tree.

She always accompanied Becky when she took the key from the kitchen shelf – the beer-barrel had to be locked up lest the Irish should get to it – and turned the tap to fill the big wicker-covered bottles.

Then came a time of waiting for the Irishmen to appear. Tom Garland scanned the sky and read the weather signs, he noted the direction of the wind and its changes, he tapped the barometer in the hall, and looked at the sky at night. He walked through the fields and rubbed the grasses between his fingers. He shook his head over the crops on the steep high fields, where tall grasses and dog-daisies hid the scanty growth beneath. He thanked God for the heavy crops on the lower fields, on the gentle slopes and by the streams.

The grass was ripe for cutting, the weather seemed likely to be fine. Everything was ready for the Irishmen, and a rumour came that they had been seen, they were near.

CHAPTER 20

The Harvest

ONE day Roger barked with more than his accustomed fury, galloping in a semicircle by the rose trees and barn, as he strained towards the hill and some distant sound.

'There's summat up,' observed Joshua to Dan, 'I shouldn't be surprised if it's the Irish.' He walked over to the bank and looked down the hill. A little procession of men swayed slowly up among the fragrant gorse and bushes of wild roses which lined the path. In their hands they carried bundles, in red and blue handkerchiefs, more baggage was slung on their backs, on rough sticks, and great loaves of bread were tucked under their arms. They smoked and spat, and waved their hats to Joshua as he leaned over the wall to greet them.

Tom came hurrying out when Dan ran breathless with the news, 'The Irish are here, they've come, Master.' The big gate opened and the file of men came straggling past the garden into the yard, down the path to the kitchen door, to pay their respects. Old Mike came first with his blue bundle in his thin brown hand. He was a small wiry man, with a face bright and keen as a bird's. He had piercing blue eyes under bushy eyebrows, uneven blackened teeth, and a pointed chin covered with stubble. He was a hard drinker and a hard worker, the men's acknowledged leader and arbitrator, a great talker and a fighter and dancer. It was he who settled the men's wages with Tom Garland, and arranged the hours of work and the terms for wet days.

His place was on the haystack, to receive the hay from the great piled wains, pitched to him with the longest forks, for he could make a cleaner, tidier, and firmer stack than anyone in the countryside. When Old Mike had finished, his stacks looked like houses, with straight sides and neat gables, a particularly difficult task where the ground sloped and dipped as it did in the stack-yard.

His father had worked at Windystone, and his grandson would come in a few years to take his place. He intended to mention him to Tom in good time.

Over a blue and white shirt, open at the neck, showing his hairy chest, he wore an old coat, green with age, a cast-off from the farm years ago. It was made of good strong broadcloth, and would last for many a season yet, but he expected with luck to get another for best from the farmer this year. His trousers were strapped at waist and ankle, and on his head he wore a black clerical hat, whose history was unknown, but he had worn it before Margaret was married, in rain, wind, and sun, for many a year. It was inseparable from him, the badge which he removed perhaps when he slept, but certainly not during the day.

As he sat on the dresser with his back to the lustre jugs and priceless old china, sipping a basin of tea, and blowing the curling steam, a strong heady smell came from him in waves, travelling up to the ceiling and into every cranny and nook of the room, a smell of tobacco twist, corduroy, beer, and Ireland. Susan called it 'The Irishmen's Smell', and sniffed it up eagerly with mingled fear and delight.

After Old Mike came Young Mike, his son, a man in middle life, as silent as his father was talkative, an indeterminate man with a faint smile, not a particular friend of anyone's, for he didn't work as hard as his father.

Malachi and Dominick, the twins, were slim young hay-makers, good-looking, curly-haired, brown-skinned, with white even teeth and broad happy smiles. They were everybody's favourites and were a constant source of fun, they were so much alike. They kissed Susan, the only men whom she allowed that privilege, and gave her a penny with the Irishmen's smell all over it, which she kept in a little box, safe with its penetrating odour, to remind her of them when they were far away.

They asked after the Master's rheumatism, and told Margaret that she got younger every year. They smiled at Becky and joked her, as she hurried backwards and forwards between kitchen, pantry, and dairy, and out to the troughs. They patted Roger who quickly stopped barking and fawned upon them.

Next came Sheumas, old, quiet, dreamy, with a gentle smile and far-away look. He was polite and timid, he drank very little and guarded his money most carefully to take back to Ireland. He looked frail, yet he worked longer than anyone. Tom thought he was a bit soft in the head, he was always the last, 'like a cow's tail', yet he was a good worker, clean and thorough.

The most important of the men were Patrick and Corney and Andy, the mowers. They were big, broad-shouldered, red-bearded men, relations of one another, brothers and cousins, quiet and courteous, but suddenly turning fierce and quarrelsome without any warning as they talked in Gaelic to one another. They were Susan's idea of brigands, or Assyrians sweeping down on the Israelites. They tied their corduroy trousers with twisted grass below the knee, to keep them out of the deep wet meadows, and at the backs of their leather belts they carried sockets holding their whetstones. They brought their own scythes wrapped in sacking on their backs.

They all crowded into the already full kitchen and ducked their heads ceremoniously as they wished, 'Good luck to ye', and 'God bless ye', and 'Here's good health'. They brought meat in the great iron pot from their Place to be cooked on the stove, and their surplus bread to be kept in the pantry, out of the way of mice or rats. Through the wide-opened door streamed the sunlight, dappling their trousers with golden discs.

The first night was spent over a few tots of beer from the barrel in the small barn. They sat outside in the evening sunshine, on long low forms near the door of their Place, telling tales of Ireland, of their wives, of the wage question, of cruel landlords and cattle-driving, and potato famine, which interested Tom extremely, and astonished Susan as she looked at their great frames and thought of the wild, savage, pagan land from which they had come, over the sea, like the summer birds.

Swallows and swifts hawked overhead, swooping down in frenzied rushes, chasing each other with shrill cries, dipping almost to the old hats rammed on the Irishmen's heads. They swept round the ancient buildings, over the grey-blue roofs, and the mossy gables with their stone balls, keeping ever near their human friends, excited and gay because the Irishmen had come and there would be companionship in the barns and cart-sheds.

The martins leaned out of their houses in the roof of the cart-shed, with their white breasts on their window-sills, joining in the cries of the birds and the talk of men.

On a high bough in the orchard sang a thrush, the same fellow who came there every night. Tom used to sit listening as he watched for the Irishmen coming and waited for the weather to become settled and the grass to ripen, and the bird sang to him alone, its long wonderful song, which he repeated under his breath in the soft whistle the animals and birds loved.

Now the men were here, and he stopped them to listen. 'Hark to the throstle yonder,' he said, and they took their pipes from their mouths and sat silent whilst the bird sang, and the great moon came slowly from behind the wood, so near, only just across a little field.

Dusk fell, and bit-bats came from the old cart-sheds below the gate, perched on the side of the hill in a sheltered ledge. They hung all day in the roof, above the plough, the chain harrow, the scarlet bonny rake, the rollers, and the deep blue and red hay-wains, but at night they came to hunt with the late swallows.

Susan waved her pinafore, to make them come to her

hands, for she always wanted to catch one of these strange, wild, night creatures. They shot past her face, squeaking their tiny high cry, and their leather wings beat softly in the air, almost noiseless, but clear to her intense senses. She could see their unblinking eyes as she stretched out her hands, but they never stopped for her to catch one.

A night-jar whirred on the ground under the sycamore

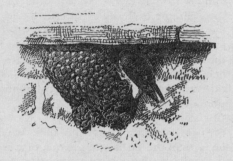

trees, and the moon rose high in the sky, shining through the dark firs.

'Good night, Dominick, good night, Malachi. Sweet repose, think of me, when you're under the clothes,' she called out as she went reluctantly to bed.

No candles were needed and as Susan undressed in the moonlight she smiled happily to think of the hay-makers and all the delight they were about to bring to the farm.

Becky, too, later on, in her little attic in the gable, looked at the moon through the skylight and sighed over Dominick's bright eyes and Malachi's gay smile, and the easy country ways of her oatcake man, who certainly couldn't say the flattering things the Irishmen said.

Mrs Garland prayed long on her knees by the bed, with her hands folded on the patchwork quilt. She prayed for fine weather, for a speedy harvest, and God's blessing on the hay.

Tom Garland lay thinking of his fields, the Daisy Spot,

with its rich heavy crop, the Ten-acre, of which the half on the high hillside was so short that it would barely pay for cutting. He thought of Whitewell field, with its hollows and hills, covered with sweet good grass, and Woodside, where the pheasants had made such havoc, trampling the grass with their long feet, of Top Pasture and Bottom Pasture, always fallow, of Harrowpiece, of Greeny Croft, and Silver Field, and Longside, and Four-ellums.

He turned uneasily as he thought of his own father, and his grandfather, lying in the same bedroom, planning, struggling through the years, from birth to death, ploughing, harrowing, harvesting.

There was little profit, but a blessed peace in this world high up, away from mithering blustering folk.

Old Joshua lay in his little room, listening to the owls which hooted over the barn roofs. The scent of honeysuckle poured in at his open window, bringing a sweet pain to his heart. He thought of his own farm, of his hopes at hay-time, under a moon like this. Old Mike had worked for him too, and he and his wife had prepared the little barn for his use, when he came with Andrew, long since dead. His orchard was full of bees, his garden full of roses, far more roses than even there were at Windystone, and a grand red honeysuckle poked its long streamers through his small squares of windows, with regular crowns of flowers. But bad luck had always followed him, first his wife had died, then his daughters had left him, accidents happened to his cattle, in field and wood, and he had bought a mare which turned lame the next day – all sorts of disasters came, till at last, daunted by Fate, he had sold all up and given in. Well, he was glad, life wouldn't be long now. Perhaps this would be his last harvest, and then he would go to the Lord's harvest.

In the fields life went on, under the moon's white light. Field mice ran along their tiny green tunnels under the bending grass, to their nests, hollowed out among the roots, just below the level of the cruel scythe. Rabbits, unconscious of the morrow, played in the mowing grass, sitting up to bite sweet juicy blades, listening for the fox who stole along by the edge of the wood. Little winds blew the sorrel and swept over the tightly closed silky seeds of dandelion and hawkweed. Then the moon hid behind a rainbow cloud and the world fell asleep.

Morning came, cool and sweet with bird-song and white mists. At five o'clock when the corncrake whirred in the Whitewell field and the cuckoo called on every side, the mowers were up and in the meadow. A soft rain fell, a good gentle rain, blessing the fields, and the dew lay thick over the grass. The three men stood on the path and sharpened their scythes, and Tom stood watching them. The music of the hone floated up the field, in at the bedroom windows, ringing a strange familiar note which came into Susan's dreams and made her smile in her sleep.

They took their positions, Patrick first, then Corney, and last Andy, and they stayed in this order during the whole of the mowing, each mowing his own lane through the grass, yet overlapping by the tip of the scythe, so that not a blade of grass remained. The long rhythmic swish, swish, swish, filled the air, as the three men, with bodies curved and motion even and regular, worked, their strong arms sweeping the shining blade through the silken grass. Their voices, murmuring in Gaelic, made a bass accompaniment to the treble of the scythes. Their feet swung onward in time to the cut of the scythe, and behind them they left three deep swathes, pale green, and soft-coloured as the rain. Now and again they stood upright and wiped the blade with a wisp of grass before they honed it afresh with the stone which they carried on their backs.

At seven they came back for breakfast, of bread and fat bacon which Becky had boiled the night before, washed down with a jug of strong tea, with milk and sugar. The hay-makers had breakfast with them and then went away for two days, to work on a small farm over the hill, until enough grass had been cut at Windystone.

After breakfast, when Dan had gone with the milk, Tom

and Joshua brought out the mowing-machine, clattering
and clacking from a cart-shed. Last year the farmer had
bought it, for use in the few level parts of the fields, and on
the gentler slopes. Often the wet had caught them before
the Irishmen had finished and with the machine he could
speed up the mowing. The mowers took the high steep field,
where the machine could not climb. They swept under the
hedges round the smooth meadows, where the ground always
rose steeply, they mowed over the ditches and by the
streams and springs, in soft ground and by the troughs, on
the slopes of the stiff hills, round groves of trees, and the
boles of the great isolated beeches and ashes and elms, which
stood in the fields. Most of the work was done by the
mowers, the machine could not cut clean on those curving,
steep hills.

All day they worked, returning only for meals to their
Place. The fallen grass lay in even swathes, in broad,
coloured, parallel stripes on a pale green robe, white dog-
daisies, red sorrel, purple vetch mixed with the deep blue
of wild geranium, and the yellows of buttercup and dandelion, lying on the short pale grass.

Over the horse's eyes hung a leafy branch of ash, to keep
away the flies, but the men worked on, each with his ac-
companying halo of dancing insects.

Now a rabbit darted out and the mowers dropped their
scythes with wild yells, and threw their hats at the bewildered animal which doubled backwards and forwards
among them until with bare hands they caught and
throttled it. Often a rabbit's legs were cut off with the scythe,
and then it only staggered a few yards before they killed it.
They were put beside the men's coats and carried back for
a stew. Hedgehogs, too, were caught by the busy mowers,
and roasted on little stick fires, when they tasted like
chicken.

Field-mice, long-legged frogs, solemn toads, were disturbed, and fled past Susan who hurried down to the fields
when she came home from school and ate her tea in the

grass. But sometimes a wasps' nest or even a hornet's hole turned the tables and made the Irishmen run.

Round and round went the mowing machine, encircling a piece of meadow land, and the little creatures who lived in it retreated further into the middle. The loud whirr and buzz of the machine terrified them, they knew not from which direction it came, and they lay trembling in the deep grass. As the island became smaller the mowers came up with cudgels from the wood-stack. They stood round ready for the frantic flight of the rabbits which came as the grass disappeared. There was pandemonium for a few moments, they yelled and bellowed, to confuse the lost, startled animals, and then a heap of furry bodies smeared with blood lay on the ground.

When the haymakers returned, with merry talk and much laughter, with the clinking of tin mugs, and the rattle of chains and harness, they went into the fields to ted the grass.

Days of hard work followed, long days, from dewy cool mornings before the sun rose behind the steep hills, to dusk, when the bit-bats came out and flew over the haymakers' heads. The house doors were all locked and Susan stayed away from school to her great delight to go with Becky and Margaret, each in a pink, lilac, or buff-coloured sun-bonnet, and a pale holland frock, to work in the fields. Margaret did not stay long, but Becky and Susan worked all day, running errands and haymaking. The mowers were well ahead, but the haymakers came after, tedding the grass with their forks, and spreading it to dry, then raking it into long lines, one behind another, each making his own swathes which curved over the hills, down the hollows, and up the little slopes till they faded away among the thin grass at the top.

Susan was for the first time in her life allowed to use a rake, one a little smaller than the others, which she slowly pulled over the hay, careful lest a tooth should be broken out, or a piece of hay should be left lying loose on the green grass.

In the next field the tedders were tossing, and in the field beyond the mowers were honing their scythes and then bending over their heavy grass. The sun beat down and dried the hay, bringing out the hidden scents, the clean delicious odours which so soon follow the pungent strong smell of cut grass.

So they travelled from field to field, uncovering all the hidden secrets of the individual meadows, the patch of rosy ragged robin, in the little marsh, the white pool of dog-daisies, the hedge covered with honeysuckle, the round nest of field-mice with pink, curled, little bodies, the water-troughs which had been so long unused that they were now hidden under the surrounding ferns. Susan left the hay-makers to run after the mowers, who were the first to find all the treasures, but, heedless, they moved steadily forward, and she hunted alone until her father called her back to bring him a drink.

By the open gates, where the little blue butterflies lived all the summer, on the shady side of the hedge, the drinks lay. Great old wicker-covered bottles, and a brown oval jar, covered with crosses and flowers like an embroidered quilt, were filled with beer and carried proudly by the Irish-men in the morning. By the side lay the tot, a pewter drink-ing-cup. Old Mike called the halt for a drink and Tom gave his consent, looking up to the sun, and calculating the time since the last tot. The beer was never left in the field with the men alone, after one disastrous day a few years before. Tom poured out the beer and the tot passed round, whilst the men wiped their foreheads and shook the sweat off their necks.

Tom and Joshua drank tea from a large white jug, with a cup over the top, or sometimes they had oatmeal water, or dandelion beer which Becky had made a short time before, very sweet and pleasant. Susan ran with the jug to her father and Becky, or went all the way back over the fields to the house for more. Inside it was cool and strange, the blinds were drawn in the parlours and sunlight danced through their whiteness, flickering on the furniture. The rooms were talking again, and she stopped to tell the news of the fields to the ghosts of the house, to the listening shadows, which waited expectantly when she entered. Margaret filled up the jugs, and gave her a little sugar-cone bag full of oatmeal and brown sugar from the two big glazed mugs on the pantry shelf. She took a toy spoon from her doll cupboard and ate the feast before she went out again to the fields, walking carefully and slowly lest she should spill the tea which 'swaled' in the jug.

At milking-time Dan and Joshua left off, but Tom worked with the men, only stopping for a bite of food, and then on again. The long lines were pushed downhill and made into cocks, first little ones and then two or three were joined together to form great cocks, like small stacks. If rain threatened everybody rushed to cock the hay, and sometimes days were spent cocking to keep out the wet, and tedding the hay out again to get it thoroughly dry.

Tom and Old Mike laid the straddles and prepared for the stacks. Then one fine day leading began, and the two hay-wains were brought out. Tom Garland and Dan led the two mares, Duchess and Diamond, with the loads of hay up the hills to the stack-yard where old Mike waited. When a cart was piled with a mountain of hay, ropes were thrown over to keep the load from slipping off as the mares struggled to the stack-yard.

'Pull! Pull! Pull agen! Pull agen! Agen! And agen! And agen!' sounded through the summer air like a sea-shanty as the Irishmen strained at the ropes to tighten the mass. Then the man on the top slid down and the perilous ascent began.

The two mares strained at the great load, and men pushed behind as the cart moved up the hills. Tom led one mare and Dan the other, encouraging, helping, and resting, when there was a chance in the slope of the field. Other men hung like flies on one side to keep the top-heavy load from tumbling over and falling down the field. It was always an anxious time, a slip and a man and mare might be killed. Only the steady-going mares could be used, the pony was too frisky, although she was often put between the two, when the hill was especially difficult, and the horse was needed for other work.

Sweat poured down the men's faces and splashed on the ground, their shirts were soaked, their arms were taut and knotted with thick veins. Old Mike stood high on the sweet-scented stack, watching the hay-cart appear and disappear, like a ship in a rough sea, as it climbed up hills and sank into hollows. Always the voices came through the crystal air, singing across meadow and wood:

'Dimond! Dimond! Pull! Pull! Dimond! Duchess!' The mares, with heads stretched forward and the muscles of their great flanks quivering, corded, stretched, pulled with all their might, and the men exhorted them, putting every ounce of strength to the task.

Shouting, sweating, the load reaches the top. Men pause to draw their hands across their faces and wring off the water, whilst they look at the bitter track up which they have fought their way. The mares tremble and Tom soothes them and strokes their wet sides. Then they start again, the last fifty yards up a gentler slope to the stack-yard, and everyone asks for a tot as the animals rest and eat a bundle of hay.

So it went on, and the fields were emptied of their burdens. One of the men walked up and down with the bonny-rake, collecting all the scraps left from leading and men went round the hedges cleaning everywhere up. Susan rode back each time in the empty cart, clinging to the side of the jolting wain, which jerked over lumps and into hollows and threatened to throw her out. But she sang a paean of joy, for this was the most beautiful thing in the world, better than a circus or a fair.

On Saturday nights the double doors of the big cart-shed were opened wide and the Irishmen gave a concert of song and dance.

Dominick was the chief singer, and he stood in front of the doors on the cobbles, whilst the song rolled on, verse after verse, none of which Susan understood. Then Old Mike danced, with great clatter of heels and swinging of arms. The others sat round motionless, with their eyes fixed on his feet, which twinkled in an astonishing way for one so old. They interrupted with cries of 'Bravo, bravo', and Old Mike's blue eyes stared across the fields to the beech wood as if he saw his own Galway mountains up there.

One after another they danced or sang, and joined in the merry choruses with stamping feet and shaking shoulders.

Sometimes Tom Garland brought out his concertina and played the airs they sang, or he gave them a hymn tune and they listened attentively. The darkness came down like a blue cloud, bit-bats flew in and out of the pitch-black shed, and screech-owls hooted in the fir trees. In the nearest fields, pale green and emptied of hay, the mares could be heard softly whinnying with pleasure, as they took their week-end rest. They knew as well as anyone that whatever the weather, however urgent the need for speed in the harvesting, nothing would be done on Sunday and they were free.

Becky sat with Susan on the wall joining in a hymn, clapping and listening to the concert which was the only kind she knew.

On Sundays the men fetched buckets of hot water from the kitchen boiler and borrowed razors and soap. They retired to a little field, mockingly called 'The Forty-Acre Field', and there they washed their bodies, and shaved off the week's growth of beard. They put on clean shirts and trousers from their bundles, in the manger of the cow-house, and tied clean bright handkerchiefs round their necks. Then they washed their dirty shirts and hung them on the hedges and bushes to dry.

When they were clean and trim and all prinked out, they went off to Mass at a church six miles away, where the priest loved these children from over the sea, and welcomed them as they waited at the door for the fine folk to enter first.

But in the farm kitchen the great iron pot simmered and bubbled over the bright fire with the Irishmen's dinner inside, which Dominick and Patrick would soon carry to the little home in the cattle-stall.

CHAPTER 21

The Wakes

THE last load of hay was gathered amidst cheers from the men who followed it down the steep hill, bumping and shaking across the uneven cow roads, under the massive beech trees which swept up handfuls among their boughs, through wide-open gates, each of which took its toll of the hay, to the stack-yard. Dan walked the fields with the big red rake, Joshua tidied up the hedges and gateways, and Old Mike and his son put the final touches to the trim, neat haystacks, the green-gabled houses with clean stack-cloths hoisted on the tackle over their roofs, to keep them dry until they had sweated and were ready for the 'thacker'.

At the top of each stack was a little attic, left open under the transverse pole, and Susan looked up at it with her eyes wide open, expecting to see a hay man peep out to say all was well up there. Once she had been helped up to the top, and there she had sat, under the heavy cream canvas roof, with the sweet-scented floor beneath her, and soft green light all round, wrapping her in aromatic waves. She looked across the open fields to the Druid Wood with its gaunt tree on the edge of the world, at the beech woods on every side, the orchard with its green fruit peeping up the slope, and the fertile valleys deep down in the hollows. Beyond were the hills edged with black trees and ragged rocks, and beyond again, out of sight, were stretches of moors, with curlew crying plaintively among the gorse and bracken, the heather and bilberries. She was glad she lived here, on an island, in the hills, and she prepared to play Robinson Crusoe in the ship as the canvas flapped round her. But at that moment, Tom looked up and saw her small face peering out of the dark-shadowed triangle.

'Coom down, you naughty lass. Whoever let you get up there was clean daft. You might fall and break your neck.'

He climbed up the long ladder and carried her down to safety.

'Never let me see you up there again, and be off home and help your mother. This is no place for you.'

That night they had the harvest supper, beer and beef and pasties, in the cart-shed, with candles stuck in the walls, lighting up their strong faces and hairy necks, twinkling against the shafts of the brightly varnished milk-cart in the background, and the heavy harness on the wall.

Bats and moths flew in and out, and loud laughter rang down the garden, and over the new green fields to the happy cattle who had come to their own again. From across the grass it looked like a scene out of a play, a theatre interior with only the dark trees as audience and the thin crescent moon the light in the roof, turned down for the play to begin.

Susan hovered about the doorway, Becky brought out some cheese, and Margaret came to see they had all they wanted. Tom stood with his hands behind his back, chatting and enjoying himself. A weight was off his mind, the rain had kept off, and the crop was fairly good. Not like two years ago when it rained for weeks, and the men left good hay to turn black in the fields, only fit for bedding, whilst they did odd jobs, mended walls, cut hedges, and hung about in the cart-sheds, with sacks on their shoulders and watched the streams of rain ruin all. One thin field they had even left uncut, and he had to buy tons of hay to last through the winter. But he had known it would be fine to finish up this year, for on St Swithin's Day he had gone out in the early morning to watch for the sun. The Irishmen were all in the fields, but he was anxious about the weather.

The rounded cherry trees, like nosegays of pointed leaves, each leaf a curved spout for the dew, were bright with red cherries, and he shouted at the blackbirds and starnels which fluttered among them, wasting as much fruit as they ate.

The apple trees, with irregular green apples slightly flushed with brown where they faced the south, clustering in twos and threes along the branches in the orchard, like love-birds with their heads under their wings, filled the orchard, rustling their boughs together, so that the roof was green.

He had sat there alone, looking for the sun. It came from behind a cloud and sent long straight rays dazzling through the foliage. He stood a moment looking at it, with thankfulness in his heart, and then went indoors.

'It's all right,' said he. 'It's all right,' he cried to Margaret. 'The sun's through the apples, we shall have a good crop, and if rain keeps off today we shall get the harvest in.'

It had kept dry, and the harvest was safely gathered, but no one knew what was in store. He went through life prepared for good or evil, taking what was given, losing today and gaining tomorrow, accepting all with cheerfulness.

After supper the men dragged the forms outside and gave their last concert. The mowers had gone some time before, and these men would follow them to the great farms in the east before they went back to Ireland.

The next morning everyone was up at dawn, to say good-bye. They stood in a group with their clothes tied up neatly in their bundles, saying the last few words. Susan nearly cried, she loved them so much, and now they were going.

Everyone said, 'Next year, next year,' and the swallows echoed, 'Next year,' as they skimmed over the barns, but Margaret whispered, 'If all's well.'

Susan stood on the bank with her mother, waving her hand to the men as they lurched down the hill, turning to wave back and shouting blessings as they went round the corner which hid them from view. She walked slowly, twisting her pinafore, into the Irishmen's Place for a final smell. Dan carried out the bags and benches, Tom put away the picture, and they prepared the cow-stall for the Alderney which was due to calve in a few days.

Susan quickly recovered her spirits, there were the wide fields all waiting for her to visit them, and the trees eager for a talk. She took her skipping-rope and raced down the prickly cut grass to the hedges and the giant trees by the gates. She visited every corner and every tree that week after school, and told her stories, and practised her new learning upon them.

Mrs Garland took her to tea on Saturday with Mrs Wolff at Oak Meadow Farm, for the harvest was finished there, too, and it was a time of rejoicing and tea parties.

The garden at Oak Meadow was very lovely, for roses grew like weeds; great dark roses like wine, and pale pink ones like airy ladies in silken dresses, red moss roses actually enclosed in wreaths of moss, and white roses, heavy and mysterious, as if they held something inside their petals, a gold heart or a green elf. Susan was going to look, if they left her alone.

There was a spring jutting up in the garden, to the water-trough, clean fresh water, which Miss Mary took her to see. All round were bright stones, little blue and green pieces of china and glass, bits of flowery plates, a patchwork of pottery and a china man with a flute among them, all hiding among ferns and moss, like a votive offering to the goddess of the water.

There were marigolds, the first Susan had seen, with seeds like little green cheeses, and petals like an angry sun. There were rows and rows of skeps, far more than at Windystone, and the air was full of little hums and talks and murmurs. The barns were thatched with straw, the cow-places huddled together, as if they were whispering secrets, as well they might, they had stood there among the oak trees so long. They were all as clean as a pin, for Miss Mary, Mrs Wolff's old daughter, bright-eyed, red-cheeked, particular Miss Mary, who was forty if she was a day, ran after each cow with a brush and a cloth, so everyone said.

Susan loved Miss Mary, but she had never been quite comfortable with Mrs Wolff since she had first suspected her of eating lambs, and young children. There might easily be a wolf under the old lady's flowered petticoats and little tight bodice, for she was like the one which ate Red Riding-hood's grandmother, and sat up in bed. It happened at Oak Meadow, and Susan did not care to be alone there.

There was also a picture in Mrs Wolff's capacious neat kitchen, a picture Susan feared, it reminded her of that hell which she contrived so often to forget. It was the Tree of Life and Death, an enormous green tree, with its roots in hell, and horrible fruit of drunkenness and many vices which Susan couldn't understand, hanging on every outstretched bough.

But the tea was good, the little cakes and jam turnovers, the damson cheese and cream, which she ate as she listened to Miss Mary and Mrs Wolff tell Margaret all the news of the life to come, of the wicked theatres they had seen on their holidays, and the bold brazen wench who had stayed at their lodgings.

But, 'Little pitchers have big ears', and Susan was sent out to the garden, free to wander among the flowers and orchard trees until Margaret came out and they walked across the field paths and through the coppice towards their own home again.

Holidays came and Susan celebrated them by going down to the station every morning in the milk-cart, and sitting quietly in the little station yard among the many carts of the neighbouring farmers, who sent their milk for miles, whilst the milk-churns were rattled and banged across the railway line, and the train came slowly puff-puffing to a standstill. She stared at the travellers whom she could see from the cart, stout women going early to market, with baskets of fowls, big men with heavy sticks in their hands, going to buy calves and pigs, and spruce little men who were out for orders for cake and grains and meal.

The train steamed away, and Dan returned and drove

home again. She had seen a little of the big world, as much as she would see, for no one from Windystone intended to go away for a holiday. They had fresh air enough, God knows, and plenty to eat and drink, and a tea party now and then, and soon the fair was coming to Mellow. What more could they want?

So Susan spent her days in the fields and garden, making scent from the rose leaves which lay in carpets of red and cream on the grass-plots, adding a little spring water and bottling them in small medicine-bottles she found in one of the lofts. The smell was never quite right, but she hoped for the best and tried again. She returned to Robinson Crusoe, and played the solitary game which never staled, in the stack-yard, or on the grass-plot with the monkey tree for the look-out, and the stone chamber for her cave. She made a haystack of pulled grass for Robinson Crusoe's fiery onager, Fanny, which ramped and curveted in the small croft, and she fed her on windfalls from the tall lonely apple tree. She shot pirates and cannibals with her father's walking-stick when they came creeping from behind the trees. She accompanied Becky to a prayer-meeting at her chapel and went with Tom to a cattle market.

Then Job Fletcher, the thatcher, came to do the stacks. He made the haystacks into well-roofed houses, which looked as if they were built to last for years. He was a talkative old man, whose head 'wasna dazed by the heights', and he worked with much pride and satisfaction at his job. 'There's nubbody can thack like me,' he said many a time, and Susan stood below near the wood-pile watching him with a peg in his mouth and the tarred thacking-twine on the wooden sticks in his fingers as he deftly twisted the line round the bright new straw. The smell of the twine and the hay kept her near like a bee at a honey-pot.

At every gable he made a stiff little bunch like a turret, or a sheaf, and tied it round its middle with straw, to bring good luck to the stack, to keep it from fire, lightning, and tempest, and when it was finished Susan looked up and saw these little messengers like angels on the roof, yellow against the blue sky. Job had a drink of beer and a couple of rabbits to take home with him when he straddled stiffly down the ladder and straightened out his legs.

School began and the days passed too quickly into the colours of autumn. First a bough on a beech tree and a cluster of leaves on an oak brought the message that the back-end was approaching. The golden splashes spread, nuts ripened, green walnuts fell from the great trees, apples reddened in the orchard and garden, the brown pears on the house were ready for picking.

Becky had a letter from the oatcake man asking her to go with him to the Wakes on Saturday.

'Can I go, Missus?' she asked Margaret, proudly holding out the note addressed to Miss Rebecca Moss.

'Yes, when you've finished your work, and suckled the calves,' answered Margaret, laughing, 'and you can take Susan with you.'

All the week Susan and Becky thought of Saturday. Each night they walked across the fields and looked over the valley to the dim mist in the folds of the hills where Mellow lay. Now a glow like a powder of gold hung in the air above the masses of trees, and when the wind was very still they could hear hoots and trumpets, faint and far-away like the sounds of gnats in the sky.

Dan brought news of the fair, of the fine dobby horses, and a merry-go-round bigger than ever, with ostriches as well as horses. He went down there at night when he had finished. He swilled his face at the slop-stone till it shone in the firelight. He rubbed sweet-smelling oil on his hair, and parted it carefully at the side before the little rose-framed mirror. He put on a clean pink-and-white rubber collar, and carried a stick in his hand, and a rose in his cap. Becky's work was never done and she looked enviously at him. Even old Joshua went down one night, and Tom Garland drove through to have a look at things.

'There's a fat woman,' he said triumphantly when he

returned, 'with arms near as big as my thighs, and a head like a great pudding. She's a comfortable-looking body, though, in spite of her fat. And there's a calf with two heads, and a chicken with four legs, and a kind of little theaytre where they act Pepper's Ghost, as I've seen many a time.'

Susan's eyes were agog with excitement, and she hurried through the wood each night hoping she would live to see the wonders, praying little prayers for safety, and stepping like a feather on the soft leaves and earth between the stones.

Becky's thoughts were on the oatcake man. Would he ask her to wed? Of course not, she hadn't known him long enough, but she would be with him and perhaps he would treat her to the swing-boats.

The day came at last, and Becky went upstairs to change to her blue silk body and her black skirt with braid round the bottom, although Margaret protested she was too grand for the Wakes. Susan wore her brown coat with astrakhan trimmings, and her last year's beaver hat. Mrs Garland had decided to go with them to bring-Susan back when Becky was with Gabriel Thorn. She packed a bottle of cream, and a pot of potted meat and a few apples for an old friend in the village in the basket which Becky carried on her arm.

They had an early tea and left the table set for the milkers, milk and sugar in the cups, a plate of thick bread and butter, a pot of marrow jam, and in the oven a dish of stewed pears and cloves, for Tom and Joshua, and Dan's tea on the dresser end.

Margaret looked back to see if everything was there, the teapot on the hob, the chairs drawn up ready. Becky made a roaring fire, and Susan ran to her father to ask for a penny to spend.

'Goodbye, goodbye. Take care of yourselves. Don't be late,' he called. 'Tell the oatcake man we shall expect some oatcakes for nothing.'

Messages floated from them as they went down the hill. 'Don't forget the stewed pears.'

'Don't give Dan any marrow tonight, he has cake.'
'Don't forget to send Joshua to meet us up the hill.'
'Don't forget to send the lantern.'

'Be off with you all,' came roaring from the farmer, who looked at the sky, and noted the curly wind clouds sweeping its great heights. Then he turned back to the house with his hands behind his back.

They walked by the rippling river, Susan in the middle, giving a little skip to keep up with them. A cart rattled by and then drew up.

'Would you like a lift?'

They gratefully accepted and climbed in, squeezed three on a seat with Susan on Becky's knee, and the basket on the floor. The horse was a spanking beast, a high stepper, with clicking hoofs, and the noise, as they rattled along, drowned the music of the river. They flew past the water-mill, with its dripping wheel, the old ivy-covered toll-gate, and the church. Susan looked up at the rooks wheeling overhead to the elms, the ducks in the backwater, sailing with ruffled feathers like white-sailed ships, the robin on the yew hedge round River Cottage, the elm tree like an immense monkey, delightful by day, but terrible and menacing at night.

On they dashed and Susan and Becky held their hats from flying away, and Margaret put up a hand to her little velvet bonnet.

They turned the last corner, and the horse was pulled up sharply before the 'Green Man'. 'Whoa, steady there, whoa,' shouted their unknown driver, for it was startled by the noise of rifles in the shooting booths, the chuff-chuff-chuff-chuff of the little engine, the music and the shouts.

They climbed down with the cart swaying and backing, as the restive horse struggled to get away. They called their thanks and the man touched his cap and smiled as he drove away from the village along a road to the right.

Mrs Garland settled her bonnet and Becky pulled down her skirts and shook herself.

The open market-place was packed with a large merry-go-round, all gold and glitter, and a small one for little children. Stalls stood along the pavements pressed close to the baker's and tin-smith's and cobbler's shops. The druggist looked out from his embrocations and bottles to the shooting-booth, and the little bow-windowed draper's shop was near the fat lady's tent and Pepper's Ghost. In front of the blacksmith's forge were the swing-boats; from ancient time they had their stand there, for the forge was low and the boats could swing out to the overhanging elms. Old gabled houses, now turned into granaries for the corn-chandler, looked on with sightless windows, through which bags of grain like fat white women peered down at the unaccustomed life below.

Margaret and Susan strolled through the village, with Becky behind with the basket. They bought brandy snap and peppermint rock, gingerbread men with currant eyes and candied peel mouths, and Wakes cakes, spiced and sugared with caraways on the top. Then Margaret gave Becky a shilling to spend at her discretion on Susan and herself and walked through a little green gate, up a narrow path edged with chrysanthemums, knobbly and small, and dahlias, red, orange, and yellow, to a green door. She tapped at the brass knocker and a white-capped maid opened, and the house swallowed her up.

Susan looked after her. She saw the sitting-room with its canary and fierce little dog which never made friends, the wax flowers under the glass shade, the carved box which was sent from Norway, the fireside with gleaming brass fender, and the old lady herself with her lace cap and purple ribbons.

But the fair called her, and the dobby horses. She and Becky stood waiting till the horses and the wonderful fierce-eyed ostriches stopped, and then they climbed up. Round and round they went, never getting off when the music stopped, but waiting proudly above the heads of the staring crowd below.

There the oatcake man found them and paid for further rounds. The music ran in Susan's head, the smooth dobby horse was cool and beautiful under her fingers, she felt herself a queen. She had nothing to do with the ostriches, they were too outlandish and foreign.

In a dream she watched the shooting, and the oatcake man tried his solitary hand at coconut shies and Aunt Sally's. Susan's thoughts were with the roundabouts and she watched her own steed with a stout party on his back, and knew he wanted her to come and talk to him again. But the oatcake man led them on to the fat woman, the calf with two heads, and Pepper's Ghost, which frightened Susan so that she pinched Becky's fingers, and frightened Becky so that she forgot her modesty and clasped Gabriel's hand.

'It's not real,' he explained in a lordly way, 'it's only illusion, done with looking-glasses and such.' But it made it worse, that a harmless looking-glass could do such a thing as show a spirit, one of the dead-and-gone. Becky and Susan had always known there was something queer about a looking-glass in which you could see behind you. They were relieved to come out and walk round the booths, where the oatcake man bought trinklements for Becky and a toy flat-iron for Susan.

Night dropped down from the overhanging cliffs and woods. The showmen lighted more flares, and lads and girls streamed into the market-place. Becky took Susan up to the gate of old Mrs Wheat's cottage and left her. She walked timidly up the path and rapped at the knocker. The ferocious dog barked savagely, and darted at her boots, when the old servant opened the door. It was an ordeal to go to Mrs Wheat's house, for the old lady and her maid peered through their spectacles like witches.

Their faces were kind and wrinkled like apples which had been left all winter in the apple chamber, but their eyes were so bright, and their fingers so thin, their backs were so curved and their chins so pointed, she feared they would

keep her shut up for ever in the small close rooms along
with the stuffed birds, the yellow canary, the wax flowers
and the carved box.

She sat on the edge of a chair, dangling her legs away
from the snuffling dog and waiting for her mother, who was
still drinking a cup of tea and talking about the church
bazaar.

Susan sighed, she wanted to go home now, she was tired,
and the striped sugar sticks were stickily waiting to be eaten
on the dark roads. She stared round the room and sighed
again. At last Mrs Garland arose and put on her bonnet
and coat. Susan shuffled off her seat and stood up on one
leg with her hand held out. She hoped Mrs Wheat would
not kiss her, with her thin lips and the beaky nose so near,
but her wishes were vain. She was kissed and her height, age,
and general attainments discussed, and all the time the
tantalizing music blazed outside, and rockets flew up among
the trees, and girls squealed with happiness.

Susan breathed deeply as they stepped out of the stuffy
house into the cold fresh air, leaving the witches behind.
The fair welcomed them, but Margaret kept close to the
pavement, and hurried through the people with Susan
dragging back. As they passed the swing-boats they saw
Becky and the oatcake man flying up to the sky.

They left the light and splendours behind them and
walked along the dark roads with no light, not even a star.
Their eyes, at first dazzled by the change, got used to the
blackness. The shapes of trees and haystacks and a wayside
cottage loomed out at them. On a window blind Susan
saw a cage with a ruffled little bird asleep on his perch, and
the sound of a concertina came softly through the door.

'Mr Samson playing a hymn,' remarked Margaret, turning her head. 'He doesn't hold with Wakes' Week, he says
it brings folk to hell.'

The woods dropped down to the roadside and they
walked by the river which shone like a snake in the darkness.
Susan could see the monkey elm tree against the sky, its arms

outstretched as if to spring. She said nothing but turned round until it was out of sight in the curve of the road.

A tiny light came wavering and flickering towards them. 'There's Joshua with the lantern,' cried Susan, and they hurried forward to save his legs. They climbed the long hill, winding where the horses winded, looking down on the tops of trees, and the curving river which flowed round a loop before it disappeared far away behind another hill.

The darkness lightened and stars came out. They passed a group of horses which sought companionship, leaning over the walls with noses touching and eyes faintly luminous in the rays of the lantern.

Like a lighthouse on an island, they saw the farm shining down on them, with its lamp among the planets. Susan walked with her head in the air watching the light and the mass of chimneys which stood out against a cluster of stars.

Everything seemed to move. The chimney-stacks swept across the Great Bear, the Pleiades were entangled in the elm's boughs, a shooting star fell with a trail of gold, the trees dropped lower and lower as they climbed above them.

Windystone floated in the air.

'It's all moving,' whispered Susan, 'moving on and on,' and she felt as if wings were behind her which would carry her away, too.

But down there waited the Dark Wood, with twisted trunks of oak and fountains of birch, with elephant beeches and knotted ash, alive and powerful.

She ran in front and opened the big white gate. Then she let it crash behind her, echoing across the hills, to tell Them she was safe.

This Peacock book is one of a new series designed to appeal to older boys and girls. We should be glad to hear if you have enjoyed it and to receive your suggestions for other books which you would like to see in this collection. On the next page you will find a list of the Peacock titles already published

Other titles in the Peacock series